Linton Hall Military School Memories

Volume 2

Linton Hall Military School Memories

Volume 2

Linton Hall Cadet

Scrounge Books
Arlington, Virginia

Copyright © 2025 Linton Hall Cadet

No part of this book may be used or reproduced, stored in a retrieval system, in whole or in part, in any manner, or transmitted in any form or by any means, electronic, mechanical, photocopying, recording, scanning, or otherwise, with the exception of brief quotations embodied in news articles, critical articles, and reviews, without the express written permission of the copyright holder.

Certain chapters in this book were previously published on the blog lintonhallmilitaryschool.blogspot.com and have undergone revision for this book:
    Copyright © 2016 Linton Hall Cadet: Chapters 2, 3, 4, 5, 6
    Copyright © 2017 Linton Hall Cadet: Chapter 7
    Copyright © 2018 Linton Hall Cadet: Chapters 8, 9, 10
    Copyright © 2024 Linton Hall Cadet: Chapters 11, 12, 13, 14

The Scripture quotations contained herein are from the New Revised Standard Version Bible, copyright © 1989, Division of Christian Education of the National Council of Churches of Christ in the U.S.A.. Used by permission. All rights reserved.

Book and cover design by Linton Hall Cadet

Published by Scrounge Books

ISBN 978-1-0691142-0-4
Library of Congress Control Number 2014934259
First edition

The events described in this book were observed or experienced firsthand by the author, and were typically witnessed by thirty to two hundred cadets, and are described precisely as the author remembers them.

The opinions expressed herein are solely those of the author, and do not necessarily reflect the views of the Benedictine Sisters of Virginia, Linton Hall Military School, Linton Hall School, its staff, faculty, or current or former students.

Publisher's Cataloguing-in-Publication Data

Linton Hall Cadet (pseud.)
    Linton Hall Military School Memories Volume 2 / Linton Hall Cadet
    Arlington, Virginia: Scrounge Books, ©2025.
    vi, 102 pages: illustrations, portraits; 26 cm.
    ISBN 9781069114204
    1. Linton Hall Military School, Bristow, Va. – History – 1901-2000
    2. Linton Hall School – History – 1901-2000
    3. Schools – Virginia – Prince William County
    4. Catholic Schools
    5. Catholic Schools – Virginia
    6. Prince William County – Bristow – History
    7. Military Cadets – Virginia – Prince William County
    8. Boys – Education – United States
    9. Boarding Schools – Virginia – Prince William County
    10. Military Education – Virginia – Prince William County
    11. Military Education – Curricula – Virginia – Prince William County
    I. Title
    U430.L5 L56 2025
    975.527 Lin
    Library of Congress Control Number 2014934259

"Even Satan disguises himself as an angel of light.
So it is not strange if his ministers also
disguise themselves as ministers of righteousness.
Their end will match their deeds."

— 2 Corinthians 11:14-15

"For you are like whitewashed tombs,
which on the outside look beautiful,
but inside they are full of the bones of the dead
and of all kinds of filth.
So you also on the outside look righteous to others,
but inside you are full of hypocrisy and lawlessness."

— Matthew 23:27-28

Contents

1. Introduction to Volume 2 3
2. Bill Farquhar on Linton Hall History 4
3. Why Didn't Linton Hall Help Poor Children Learn a Trade? 6
4. Linton Hall's Precursor, St. Joseph Institute, in 1922 Had Flies, Bedbugs, Lice, a Typhoid Fever Outbreak … Plus a Fake Priest Having Sexual Relations With a Sixteen-Year Old Girl 9
5. Linton Hall Alumni Included Nicaraguan President's Sons 11
6. Why Linton Hall Had to Change 12
7. Linton Hall's Benedictine Tradition: the Shocking Truth 14
8. Sister Mary David, O.S.B. Writes Back 17
9. Maxime DuCharme, Linton Hall's Fourth and Last Commandant 19
10. LHMS Dress Uniform, with Photos 21
11. Col. Marlin S. Reichley, Linton Hall's Third Commandant 25
12. The Differences Among Linton Hall's Officers 26
13. Sister Mary David, O.S.B 31
14. LHMS Videos on Youtube.com 32
15. Military Day, 1948 35
16. Military Day Address, 1950 37
17. Lt. Lawrence Scott Carson, Jr., Linton Hall's Second Commandant 40
18. "Whatever I was doing, I was doing it for God because He wanted me to do it." – Sister Mary David, O.S.B 42
19. Photos 43

20. Bill Farquhar, Gym Teacher and Coach 46
21. More About Linton Hall Alumnus John Phillips
    of The Mamas and the Papas 47
22. Linton Hall During the Mid-1970s 49
23. Father Blase Strittmatter, O.S.B. 51
24. Punishments 53
25. School and Teachers 62
26. Memories, Updates and Thoughts 65
27. When Nobody Cares 73
28. Out of Bounds: Linton Hall Buildings 77
29. Benedictine Vows and the New 'Monastery' 79
30. Should Nuns Run Military Schools? 84
31. Closing Thoughts 89
Appendix A: List of Sisters at Linton Hall Cemetery 90
Appendix B: List of Others at Linton Hall Cemetery 98
Appendix C: Linton Family Cemetery 99
About the Author 101
Back Cover Photo Captions 102

1
Introduction to Volume 2

In 2010, approximately forty years after I had graduated from Linton Hall Military School, I began to write a blog about my own experiences, as well as what other cadets had experienced. I *needed* to write the story of our years there, which had been concealed by the censorship of outgoing letters to our parents, and the revisionist whitewash of the past by the Benedictine nuns.

In 2014 I published my book, *Linton Hall Military School Memories,* to put into permanent tangible form my previous blog posts together with several new chapters. I made this book available on Amazon.com, and priced it to cover Amazon's charge for printing and selling the book, without a penny of royalty to me.

At the time, I thought I had nothing more to say. That was not the case. This second volume contains all my subsequent blog posts, as well as seventeen interesting new chapters which have not been published before and can only be read in this book. For the convenience of blog readers, the new material begins with Chapter 15.

2
Bill Farquhar on Linton Hall History

Bill Farquhar,[1] who was sports coach as well as Gym and Geography instructor at Linton Hall for several decades, was also somewhat of a history buff. In 1992, he delivered a speech on Linton Hall history.[2] Among the interesting facts he shared:

• Route 619, part of which is also known as Linton Hall Road, was a Native American trail during the pre-Colonial period. There was also a Native American campground in the portion of the Linton Hall property where Broad Run curves, and arrowheads have been found there.

• There were slaves on John Linton's land, prior to its being donated to the Benedictines for the site of today's Linton Hall School. At least eight slaves were buried there, each grave marked with a large rock. Unfortunately, around 1941-1942, the gardener, who did not know why the rocks were there, and because they made lawn mowing difficult, dug them up and buried them deeper. As a consequence, the location of those grave sites is now unknown.

• During the 1920s, farmers working on the Linton Hall Military School land found cannonballs and old shells from the Civil War. A few of these were put on display in the old convent, and when the new convent was built, Bill Farquhar was given a few. A few years after receiving them, Bill wondered whether some of them might still be live, so he contacted the Sheriff, Ralph Shumate, who called Fort Belvoir. Some soldiers came from Ft. Belvoir and put the shells in a box — very gently, because they were, in fact, live. They brought back the parts from the exploded shells about a month later.

---

[1] A biography of Bill Farquhar is featured in Chapter 20.

[2] Special thanks to the alumnus who made me aware of the existence of Bill's speech and to the Prince William County Historical Commission for having audiotaped it.

- During the 1930s, there were very few paved roads in the area. Linton Hall Road was still a dirt road, which became extremely muddy when it rained. This all changed when, in 1938, John Joseph Becker, a lawyer from Norfolk, sent his three sons to Linton Hall Military School. According to Bill, Mr. Becker used his influence with Virginia Highway Commissioner Henry G. Shirley (after whom the Shirley Highway was named) to have the road paved from Chapel Springs to Linton Hall. It was not until around 1952-1953 that the rest of Linton Hall Road, all the way to Gainesville, was paved.

3
Why Didn't Linton Hall Help Poor Children Learn a Trade?

That was, after all, the condition under which the Benedictine Order was given 1,736 acres of land by Sister Mary Baptista, V.H.M..[3]

In 1893, Sister Mary Baptista gave the land subject to the condition that it be used for

"an industrial and training school for poor and friendless white boys and youths ... [and] a school for training and education of poor and friendless white girls in habits of industry and virtue and in learning useful occupations suitable to their condition of life"[4]

In this context, the term *friendless* means children who have no parents or other relatives taking care of them — orphaned or neglected, in today's language. *Industrial, training* and *useful occupations suitable to their condition of life,* means that they were to be taught a trade, rather than an academic curriculum. The limitation to whites became unenforceable as a result of court cases and civil rights legislation.

Saint Joseph Institute was opened in 1894 and closed in 1922, as will be detailed in Chapter 4. Although a school for boys, it "was never a first-rate educational institution, and it was never really an industrial school at all." [5]

Nor was the condition that poor children attend the schools met,

---

[3] Johnston, Sister Helen, *The Fruit of His Works.* Bristow, Va.: Linton Hall Press, 1954, pp. 37-40. I recall meeting Sister Helen while I was at Linton Hall, when she substituted for another teacher once or twice.

[4] Baumstein, Dom Paschal, O.S.B., *My Lord of Belmont: A Biography of Leo Haid.* Belmont, N.C.: Herald House, 1985, p. 138, quoting Archives of the Abbey of Maryhelp, Deed from Phillips to Trustees, January, 1893. Baumstein's meticulously researched book, although dealing primarily with Belmont Abbey and Abbot Haid, devotes one chapter to the Linton legacy.

[5] Baumstein, op. cit., p.151.

at least not as a general practice. There was strong resistance to covering the costs of poor children by St. Joseph Institute, which requested payment by the Diocese of Richmond for those boys.[6]

In 1894, the Benedictine Sisters opened Saint Edith, an academy for girls. In 1897 they opened Saint Anne, an industrial school for girls.[7]

The girls' schools founded by the Benedictine Sisters were not built on the 1,736 acres of land from Sister Mary Baptista's bequest, but on the nearby 92.5 acre Kincheloe farm, which had been originally owned by the Linton Family and sold off, and which was then purchased by the Benedictine Sisters. As this land was not part of the Linton gift, the sisters were not bound by the conditions placed on the Linton bequest.[8]

However, it could be argued that, in spirit, the condition of building a girls' industrial school had been met. But the girls' schools in Bristow were closed when Linton Hall Military School was opened in 1922.

It is not known whether or not St. Anne requested diocesan support for girls' expenses, but in 1922, with Saint Joseph Institute continuing to insist that it would only accept orphans if the diocese paid their fees, Bishop O'Connell became concerned that the trust agreement was being violated, and the Benedictines risked losing the property.[9] This matter came to a head with a court case in the Prince William County (Virginia) Circuit Court in February 1923. Although the Diocese of Richmond argued that because there was no industrial school, and the instruction was educational rather than industrial, and the monks declined to take "friendless" boys free of charge, the terms of the trust had been violated. St. Joseph Institute, on the other hand, argued that because no protest had been lodged within twenty years, it was too late to enforce the trust's provisions. The court ruled in favor of St. Joseph's, and title to the land passed to the Benedictines free and clear, with Sister Mary Baptista's conditions no longer in place. Four years later, in 1927, the Belmont Abbey gave the 1,736 acres of land, together with buildings thereon (except for the library and its contents) and livestock to the Benedictine Sisters.

As a result, Sister Mary Baptista Linton's gift became property of the Benedictine Sisters, even though no industrial school for boys and youths was ever built, and the girls' industrial school, Saint Anne, was in

---

[6] Ibid, pp.160-161.

[7] Ibid, p.149.

[8] Johnston, op. cit., pp. 51-52.

[9] Baumstein, op. cit., pp. 172-173.

existence from 1897 to 1922 — a period of only twenty-five years.[10] Most of this land was later sold off to developers by the Benedictine Sisters, and the extensive land on which Linton Hall Military School alumni went camping and hiking is no longer owned by Linton Hall School. As of 2024, the Benedictine Sisters own only 91 acres in Bristow, having sold off about 95% of their previous landholdings.

I do not know how the proceeds of the land sale were used, or whether they were used in line with Sister Mary Baptista's wishes.[11] I believe that although there was no legal obligation to do so, a moral obligation existed.

---

[10] Ibid, pp. 174-175.

[11] Chapter 29 describes how the sale of a portion of the land was used to build the expensive new "monastery."

4
Linton Hall's Precursor, St. Joseph Institute, in 1922 Had Flies, Bedbugs, Lice, a Typhoid Fever Outbreak ... Plus a Fake Priest Having Sexual Relations With a Sixteen-Year-Old Girl

A scathing report by Joseph Tobin, O.S.B. written on August 4, 1922, described extremely filthy conditions at Saint Joseph Institute, the boys' boarding school run by Benedictine priests and brothers in Bristow, Virginia.

Frater Tobin, an undercover investigator sent by Abbot Leo Haid, O.S.B., of Belmont Abbey, N.C., described a deplorable lack of hygiene, with bedbugs, lice, and a refectory "infested with flies." His report also stated that a water inspector had forbidden use of well water for drinking, and that the outhouse had not been cleaned in two years. A doctor and nurse inspected the premises and threatened to condemn the whole institute.[12]

The lack of hygiene had resulted in an outbreak of typhoid fever, with five boys who had stayed over the summer ending up bedridden, and at least two of them, the Barnes brothers, critically ill. Their mother was not informed of her sons' illness for eight days, and when she arrived she found her sons with "temperature[s] running at that time 105 [degrees] ... just covered with flies, lice and bedbugs." Mrs. Barnes had her sons transferred to a Washington, D.C. hospital. It is not known whether they recovered.[13]

Frater Tobin's report also confirmed concerns raised by both Mr.

---

[12] Baumstein, Dom Paschal, O.S.B., *My Lord of Belmont: An Autobiography of Leo Haid.* Belmont, N.C., Herald House, 1985, pages 166-167. An extensively documented book. Although the book deals primarily with the Benedictine's activities at Belmont Abbey, N.C., there is a chapter which covers the Linton land bequest, and the Benedictines' activities in Bristow until the founding of Linton Hall Military School.

[13] Baumstein, op.cit., pp.164-165, quoting a letter from Mrs. A.J. Barnes to Abbot Haid, dated August 3, 1922.

Barnes and by Mrs. Keane, a nurse hired to take care of the ill boys, that Denis Smith, who passed himself off as a priest, but who was not, had taken "liberties" with the 16-year-old daughter of a woman working as a cook at the Institute.[14]

The following month, Father Ignatius Remke, O.S.B., arrived at Bristow and confirmed that the reports "about the dirt, filth, etc. of this place" were "all true," and that although there were two wells, the water was unacceptable for human consumption.[15]

A year later, Father Remke discovered that a broken sewer line had been discharging human waste under the priory for up to three years.[16]

In order to restore hygiene and improve living conditions, enrollment at St. Joseph, which had previously been 77 boarding students and 11 day students, was drastically reduced to between 25 and 30.[17] At that point, Saint Joseph Institute was "allowed to die of attrition." The Benedictine sisters, who had been running two schools for girls in Bristow, Saint Edith Academy and Saint Anne, closed these two girls' schools, continued their activities teaching girls in Richmond, and opened Linton Hall Military School for boys in Bristow, Virginia. In 1927 the 1,736 acres of land donated by the Lintons were given to the Benedictine sisters.

---

[14] Ibid, p.166.

[15] Ibid, p. 172, quoting a letter from Fr. Remke to Abbot Haid, dated September 11, 1922.

[16] Ibid, p. 172, quoting a letter from Fr. Remke to Abbot Haid, dated September 26, 1923.

[17] Ibid, p. 172, quoting a letter from Fr. Remke to Abbot Haid, dated January 22, 1924.

5
Linton Hall Alumni Included Nicaraguan President's Sons

During the 1962-1963 school year, Luis Somoza, age 12, and his brother Álvaro, age 11, attended Linton Hall Military School. (I do not know whether they attended Linton Hall other years.) They were the sons of Luis Antonio Somoza Debayle, who was president of Nicaragua from September 29, 1956, through May 1, 1963. He died in 1967 (at age 44) of a massive heart attack. The boys' mother, however, lived until 2014.

The boys' grandfather was Anastasio Somoza, born 1896, and president from 1937 to 1947 and again from 1951 to 1956, when he was assassinated.

The boys' uncle (brother of their father,) Anastasio Somoza Debayle was president from 1967 to 1972 and from 1974 to 1979. He was deposed by the Sandinistas after a long civil war in July 1979. He fled to Paraguay, where he was assassinated in September 1980.[18]

The Somoza family rule over approximately four decades has been described as a hereditary dictatorship.

---

[18] Pittsburgh Press, June 28, 1963, page 2; Wikipedia.

6
Why Linton Hall Had to Change

Linton Hall School has undergone radical changes during the time since I was there. As far as I can tell, most of these changes were in response to external factors, rather than the result of a desire to change from within.

The increasing unpopularity of the Vietnam war led to a loss of prestige of the military, and this had an effect on military schools as well, although the decline in the number of military schools in the U.S. had begun even before the beginning of the Vietnam war.

At the same time, single-sex schools were also losing their appeal for reasons which included the lack of opportunity for socialization with the opposite sex, as well as the desire to give girls and women the opportunity to attend schools that had excluded them.

Although I did not care for the military aspect (I would have preferred to spend my time in better ways,) nor the all-boys aspect (I was, after all, at an age when I was experiencing a growing interest in girls) nor being in a boarding school, those aspects of the school were fully and openly disclosed. It is with the corporal punishment and other humiliation by the adults in charge with which I take issue, since not only were these excessive, but they were also concealed from parents through censorship of outgoing mail. I describe most of these punishments in Chapter 24, "Punishments."

It was in 1989 (coincidentally, the year in which Linton Hall went from being an all-boys military boarding school to a coeducational non-military day school) that the Virginia legislature passed a law, Virginia Code Section 22.1-279.1, which outlawed corporal punishment in public schools. Although the law did not apply to private schools, the tide was turning, and the corporal punishment with which many alumni were all too familiar, seemed to be on shaky legal ground.

Nine years later, in 1998,Virginia Code Section 22 40-705-30 provided a definition of abuse and neglect which I believe would encompass many of the punishments which were practiced at Linton Hall during the late 1960s. These would include any physical injuries resulting from corporal punishment (such as beatings with a wooden paddle or leather belt, or being made to chew a bar of soap) as well as the mental abuse of publicly humiliating younger children who had accidentally wet the bed by forcing them to wear their own urine-soaked pajamas tied around their neck all day.

Ironically, in 2013, fifteen years after the second of these laws was passed, the Virginia Senate passed Resolution #31 commending the Benedictine Sisters of Virginia on their 90th anniversary.

From everything I've heard (obviously, my first-hand experience at Linton Hall Military School ended when I graduated) today's Linton Hall School has vastly improved over the decades.
I cannot think of any substantial way in which I would suggest it could be improved. It is only unfortunate that it would take changes in the law to bring this about, instead of the Benedictine Sisters deciding to do the right thing on their own.

7
Linton Hall's Benedictine Tradition: the Shocking Truth

On the internet, Linton Hall School describes itself as "a Catholic school in Benedictine Tradition." So what really is this Benedictine Tradition? I doubt that most people really know; and I think it likely that most will be shocked to learn the truth.

Benedictine refers to Benedict of Nursia (480-547 A.D.) who founded a dozen monasteries near Rome. He was proclaimed a saint in 1220 and the Order of St. Benedict was named after him.

Just what were Benedict's beliefs, precepts and values? They are found in the Rule of St. Benedict,[19] which he wrote to govern behavior in the monasteries he founded. Although the original was destroyed by fire in 896, various (handwritten) copies remain, the most reliable the one kept in St. Gallen, Switzerland.

Benedict saw obedience as a master virtue, and advocated the annihilation of self will. That's right, human beings who are given free will by God should instead obey a "superior" (Benedict, for example.) Alumni of Linton Hall Military School should not be surprised by this.

To justify his Rule, Benedict selectively quotes the Bible. This reminds me of a quote in Shakespeare's "The Merchant of Venice" — "The Devil can cite Scripture for his purpose."

In Chapter 2 of his Rule, Benedict states "the proud, the disobedient and the hard-hearted should be punished with whips, even at the first signs of sin." To justify this, he cites "The fool is not corrected by words" (Proverbs 29:19) and "strike your son with rod and you shall deliver his soul from death" (Proverbs 23:14.) Needless to say, he does not explain what makes Benedict, or any abbot for that matter, qualified to whip others.

Chapter 4 contains a long list of "instruments of good works," or rules, the first seven of which rephrase seven of the Ten Commandments. Not content to quote God's words, Benedict must have thought he could do a better job restating them. Some of the gems

---

[19] Benedict of Nursia, *The Rule of Saint Benedict,* translated by Anthony C. Meisel and M. L. del Mastro. New York: Image Books / Doubleday, 1975.

written by Benedict include #11, "chastise the body," #12, "not love pleasure," #59, "despise one's own will" (presumably this does not apply to Benedict, since he believes that *his* will should be followed by the monks, for #59 states "obey the abbot's commands in all things.")

In Chapter 5 he repeats this, stating "obey any command of a superior as if it were a command of God." This ties in with Chapter 7 of the first volume of my book, "Blind Obedience."

I must point out that in the officer commission I received at Linton Hall Military School, lower-ranking cadets were required to follow only lawful commands. This limit on authority came up as well in conjunction with both the Nuremberg trials and the My Lai Massacre trial.

Benedict further states that "God will not be pleased by the monk who obeys grudgingly" (as you can see, Benedict has appointed himself as God's spokesman) and attempts to justify this statement by quoting 2 Corinthians 9:7 which states that "God loves a cheerful giver" and which refers to something entirely different than Benedict's position. In fact, 2 Corinthians 9:7 states, in its entirety, "Each of you should give what you have decided in your heart to give, not reluctantly or under compulsion, for God loves a cheerful giver."

Chapters 24, 25 and 26 advocate shunning as punishment, and the same shunning to anyone who should speak or meet with someone who is the subject of shunning.

If shunning is not enough, Chapter 28 advocates punishment by whipping, and Chapter 30 advocates enforced fasting or flogging of youths, i.e., those who are too small to defend themselves from an adult.

Chapter 33 speaks of the "vice of private ownership" and states that no one should give, receive or keep anything, not even a book, tablet or pen, and that "all things are to be common to every one," using as justification for his position the fact that the Apostles shared things. Quite a stretch between voluntary sharing and involuntary abolition of private property, it seems. He adds that "monks have neither free will nor free body." Can you get more autocratic than that? And can you get farther away from 2 Corinthians 9:7 cited above, which refers to voluntary giving and goes against both compulsion and against Benedict's contention that monks have no free will.

Benedict wasn't much of a fan of personal hygiene. In Chapter 36 he states that "The sick should be permitted baths as often as necessary but the healthy and especially all young are to bathe rarely." Well, I suppose that bathing rarely does make the vow of chastity easy to follow!

Although according to Benedict "monks have neither free will nor free body" (in Chapter 33, quoted above) Benedict says that "if one makes a mistake in chanting a psalm ... he must immediately humble himself publicly ... children should be whipped for these mistakes." (Chapter 45.)

Chapter 54 forbids the giving or sending of letters or parcels even to or from one's parents without the abbot's permission, and if any parcels are received the abbot may give them to whomever he decides. Linton Hall Military School alumni will certainly recall the censorship of outgoing (and, less frequently) incoming letters, even between cadets and their parents.

Chapter 69 advocates punishment for those who seek to defend or protect another. In other words, the virtue of compassion is a punishable offense.

In chapter 63, Benedict states that the "abbot, however, since he takes the place of Christ, shall be called Abbot or My Lord."

I believe that Benedict was quite unlike Jesus Christ (Jesus offered mercy and forgiveness) and Benedict was autocratic, self-righteous and arrogant, and does not deserve to be called a saint.

This would have made for an interesting book report for Religion class when I attended Linton Hall, don't you think?

8
Sister Mary David, O.S.B. Writes Back

I attended Linton Hall Military School while Sister Mary David was principal. Many years later she resumed use of her birth name, and became known as Sister Doris Nolte, OSB.

I believe that, as Principal, she was ultimately responsible for both the good and bad aspects of LHMS. In 2018, when I learned that she was still at the convent in Bristow, where she was involved in projects including adult literacy and training caretakers, I wrote her an email, asking for an apology. I wrote:

"Sister Doris Nolte,
I attended Linton Hall while you were principal.
Linton Hall was good academically, as were the field hikes and camping. However, punishments were cruel and excessive, including ..."

(A long summary of the punishments at Linton Hall follows.)

"Now the truth is out, shared and corroborated by many LHMS alumni, thanks to the Internet.
I don't wish for what you did to us to be done to you, since to wish that would take me down to your level.
But I do believe that a sincere, public apology from you to the hundreds of cadets who attended Linton Hall while you were principal is the least you can do, and is long overdue.
If you decide to reply, I will publish your response on the internet for all to see. If there's no reply within fifteen days, I will report that fact, and your silence will speak louder than words.
Sincerely,

*A Linton Hall Alumnus
(It doesn't matter who I am. I am one of hundreds who suffered at Linton Hall.)"*

Here is her reply:

"I'm very sorry these things happened while you were at Linton Hall. I'm not aware of all the things you spoke of, but I'm sure they were traumatic to some of the cadets. Forgive us all for the unpleasant things you experienced while a student with us. We meant no harm, but we tried, to the best of our ability, to make Linton Hall a safe and caring environment. If you wish to discuss this further feel free to visit me at the monastery here in Bristow.

*Peace and blessings,
Sister Doris (formerly Sister Mary David)"*

After much reflection, I replied:

*"Sister Doris,
Thank you for your prompt reply.
Although I would not characterize LHMS as "caring," I accept your apology and forgive you. I wish you well.
I can speak only for myself, and will share your reply with other alumni."*

9
Maxime DuCharme, Linton Hall's Fourth and Last Commandant

Maxime "Max" Louis DuCharme, Jr. who was Linton Hall Military School's fourth and last Commandant, passed away on June 8, 2018 at "22:23 Military" time (according to the death certificate) at Bozeman Deaconess Hospital in Bozeman, Montana due to a complete heart block two days before his death. He was ninety years old. Funeral services were held at 11 a.m. on June 21 at Sunset Hills Cemetery in Bozeman, Montana. Mr. DuCharme was cremated.[20]

Born on December 17, 1927, in Washington, D.C., he was a Linton Hall alumnus, having attended during seventh and eighth grade. In 1946, he graduated from Belmont Abbey, a high school founded by Benedictine monks in Belmont, N.C.. Belmont Abbey's 1946 yearbook, the Spire, below his name bears the quote "The cynosure of neighboring eyes," a quote from John Milton's 1645 "L'Allegro." He is described in the yearbook as "A happy-go-lucky fellow, handsome, plays football, and loves a good bull session. His effervescent friendliness and his gentlemanly manner [have] won many friends for him during his past four years at the Abbey. He is a cadet Lieutenant."

At age 18, after graduating from high school, he enlisted in the U.S. Marines, and trained at Parris Island, S.C. and Camp LeJeune, N.C.. As a Marine, he was sent to Trinidad, Cuba, Puerto Rico, and various European countries, and later participated in the 1950 landing in Inchon, Korea. He was later Operations Chief of the Engineering section of the Equipment Branch, and did a tour of duty on the Japanese island of Okinawa. He married and had a son, then in 1959 became a Marine recruiter in Traverse City, Michigan. He retired from the USMC with the rank of Master Sergeant. A proficient marksman, he was awarded at least two NRA medals.

---

[20] Source: Bozeman Daily Chronicle and various other sources.

Apparently he had two relatives, possibly aunts, who were Benedictines, as there are two nuns with the last name of Ducharme buried in the Linton Hall cemetery (see Appendix A.)

In 1965 he became Linton Hall's fourth and final Commandant. After the school dropped the military program, he continued at Linton Hall, teaching "Outdoor Education, Conservation and Ecology" (OECW) which apparently is quite similar to the field hikes of LHMS.

His wife, Agnes Louise, passed away in 2011 at age 80.

Below: Maxime DuCharme's draft registration card

10
LHMS Dress Uniform, with Photos

The dress uniform was worn on special occasions, most often when going home for the weekend, but also when returning from the weekend, as it would be worn for the retreat parade, which occurred just after we had been dropped off by our parents and which would be the last we and our parents would see each other until the next visit home, which typically happened every two weeks.

The uniform was also worn on the few field trips we took, on parades, as well as on Military Day, although for Military Day the uniform was slightly modified by substituting white cotton pants, called white ducks, for the woolen uniform pants. Also, on Military Day commissioned officers wore a shako — a cylindrical military hat with a set of white feathers. This hat made us officers look taller and stick out more from the rest. That hat did not belong to us, but was lent to us for the occasion, to be returned and re-used on the next Military Day.

The dress uniform was made of 100% wool and the partial lining was 100% cotton, and was tailored to fit, unlike the uniforms we wore daily, which were always too large and ill-fitting.

Because for many, or perhaps most of us, the first stop after leaving Linton Hall was to stop at a fast food place on Route 29, just after leaving Linton Hall Road and before entering Route 66, the uniform was subject to getting stained. As there was no time to get the uniform dry cleaned over the weekend, it could only be cleaned during Christmas, Easter or Summer break. Proper cleaning would have entailed removing all buttons and patches and sewing them back on, and the hat would have had to be cleaned by hand, as it had a plastic visor. I don't remember whether my dress uniform was ever cleaned, but I doubt it was, and I imagine that would be the case for many others.

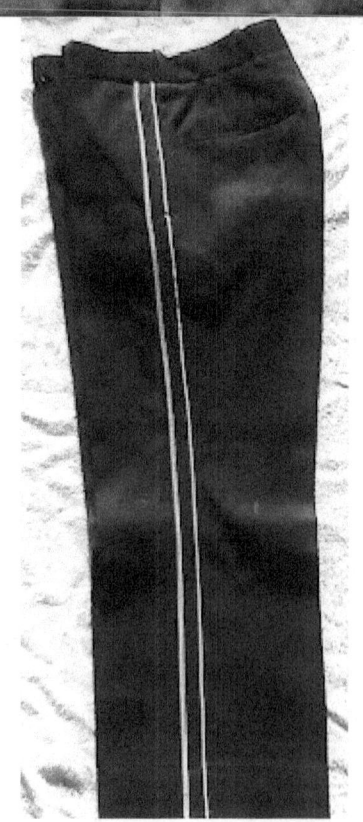

     I have to admit that I liked wearing that uniform, but only within the walls of Linton Hall and on the parade field. As soon as we left Linton Hall's driveway and turned right onto Linton Hall Road, I hated wearing that uniform, because it made me feel as if I were still there.

     My mother felt differently — and that's a huge understatement. I was made to wear that uniform at a Christmas get-together with relatives, at a wedding, and worst of all, at a funeral. In all those settings wearing the LHMS uniform was just as inappropriate as it would have been to wear a football uniform or to dress like a cowboy, indian or pirate. This is especially true at a funeral, where it would have been extremely disrespectful to call attention to myself when everyone else was dressed in black. Thank God my mother got lost driving to the funeral and we never made it.

I don't know whether God intervenes in human affairs, but if He doesn't, it was a lucky break. I wasn't told who the funeral was for, just that it was for a little child, but many years later I found out that the little sister of a girl I knew from the school I attended prior to Linton Hall had died at about the same time, so the funeral could well have been for her.

For a uniformed adult who was in the military it would have been appropriate, but for me to have been there in my attention-getting costume (not uniform) would have been a slap in the face.

Hat insignia

Collar and Lapel

11
Col. Marlin S. Reichley, Linton Hall's Third Commandant

Linton Hall's third Commandant was Marlin Sherwood Reichley, who held the position for almost thirty years.

Born in Ohio on February 2, 1915, he grew up in Sunbury, Pennsylvania, and earned Bachelor, Master and Doctorate degrees from Georgetown University in Washington, D.C. and later was a member of the university's Board. He served in the U.S. Army during World War II and the Korean war, and was employed for approximately thirty years at the Industrial College of the Armed Forces at Ft. McNair, from which he retired in 1975 as Dean of Academics.

From 1938 through the mid 1960s, he was Commandant of Linton Hall Military School.

Col. Reichley died on February 17, 1999, a few days after his 84th birthday at Powhatan Nursing Home in Falls Church, Virginia of pneumonia, after residing in the nursing home for approximately two years. At the time of his death he was a member of Resurrection Lutheran Church in Arlington, Virginia. He is buried at Arlington National Cemetery, Section 66, Site 7399.

12
The Differences Among Linton Hall's Officers

"All animals are equal, but some are more equal than others."
— Animal Farm *by George Orwell, a book we read in eighth grade English class at Linton Hall.*

Not all officers were equal. The difference was not just in rank, but in position, i.e., the role the officer played.

I've mentioned the not unusual case of an officer being demoted to Private, while keeping his position as Platoon leader or Company Commander, in Chapter 24 of my previous book ("Getting Bumped: The Officer's Rite of Passage.") On the other hand, officers of the same rank could hold positions of far differing responsibility, challenge and prestige.

The top dog (to keep the animal analogy) was the Battalion Commander, who would typically reach the rank of Major. Second only to the Commandant in power and authority, he was of unquestioned loyalty, obedience, and compliance with Linton Hall's rules. His position made him feared by everyone, including his fellow officers, and this was a double edged sword, since it also had the effect of isolating him socially from others. Whereas it was not uncommon for a Second Lieutenant to be friends with a Captain, it was difficult for anyone to let his guard down around the Battalion Commander, for fear of accidentally committing some infraction or saying something negative about Linton Hall.

Since he, as well as his adjutant and the Battalion Sergeant Major did not belong to any company, he would end up sleeping in the dormitory of one of the companies. I had the occasion to have him in my dormitory one year, so I got to observe him a lot — preferably from a safe distance, as he did not cut anyone any slack.

I am not qualified to generalize about Battalion Commanders, since there was only one each year, but I think I can safely say that they were the most loyal and most qualified leaders; I say this as someone who was not even a potential candidate for that position. Another consideration was height — which was mostly due to the Battalion Commander's age, as he was about two years older than the typical eighth grader, and had the advantage of intimidating physical size working in his favor.

Second in command to the Battalion Commander was his Adjutant. I can best compare his position as that of the Vice President of the United States. Although a prestigious position, the Adjutant had a very limited role. He only took over the Battalion Commander's duties on rare occasions, such as when the Battalion Commander lay sick in bed from the flu. Other than reporting a count of cadets, which involved adding up the numbers reported by each of the Company Commanders, the Adjutant did not do much. Don't get me wrong — I believe that the Adjutants were fully qualified to take over as Battalion Commanders — it's just that the occasion rarely arose and, given the extreme loyalty and punctiliousness of Battalion Commanders, the Adjutant had no reasonable chance of taking the Battalion Commander's spot, although typically he would be reach the rank of Captain.

The Adjutant did sleep in the same dorm I was in during one year (not the same year as the Battalion Commander) and he was very much a slacker who went with the flow, followed the rules, but did not display much motivation or ambition. That's understandable, since he had little to do and no prospects of promotion. To cite one example, it was customary to rotate the responsibility of leading the dorm in the morning activities of getting dressed, washing and making one's bed between the Company Commander, the two Platoon Leaders, and eventually the Company Sergeant. The Adjutant was also given this opportunity as a courtesy, which he declined.

The battalion also had a Sergeant Major, a seventh grader who it was tacitly understood would be Battalion Commander the following year. I believe that most would agree with me that Adjutant was a position entailing less leadership, and thus being less desirable, than either Company or Platoon Leader.

Some years there was an additional officer in battalion staff, a Supply Officer, whose responsibility was to run the arsenal, where drill rifles and camping and hiking equipment were kept. As this position dealt with equipment and not people, it required little to no leadership skills, and appears to have been given as a reward to someone who tried hard, followed all the rules, may even have been outstanding at drill, but just lacked leadership skills.

When I was at Linton Hall there were five companies: two junior companies, A and B, two senior companies, C and D, and the Drum and Bugle Corps, sometimes also known as Company E, and which was considered a senior company. Each company had three officers: a Company Commander and the First and Second Platoon Leaders.

The two junior companies had younger cadets, those in second through fourth or fifth grade, and the other companies had older cadets, generally in fifth through eighth grade. This was a general rule; those in the middle, specially fifth graders, could end up in a junior or senior company based upon their age or rank; for example, a fifth or sixth grader could end up as squad leader in a junior company, or a fourth grader who had repeated the fourth grade could end up in a senior company because of his age. The officers, however, were always eighth graders, and the sergeants typically seventh graders, in both junior and senior companies. Some of the sergeants were eighth graders.

A much-debated question, which has good arguments on both sides, is whether it was more difficult, and thus more prestigious, to be an officer in a junior or senior company. On the one hand, it may seem easier to be an officer in a junior company, since the major advantage in age and size made an officer more intimidating to younger cadets, even though officers were not allowed to use corporal punishment. (As an aside, I agree that it would have been wrong for a 13-year old officer to hit a younger child. Yet why was it allowed for a 40-plus year old man or woman to repeatedly strike a child with a wooden paddle or leather strap?)

On the other hand, although older cadets were much less likely to be intimidated by an officer's size, they were better able to understand the consequences of demerits and court martials.

As to drill, it was more challenging to deal with younger cadets, who had not yet developed the motor skills, or ability to understand the details of the various commands. This became very clear to me one time when supervising third grade study hour (officers were rotated among the different grades, so each of us had the opportunity to supervise cadets of the various grades.) There was a third grader who, although trying his best, would get right and left confused. I realized that he was well-intentioned and tried to explain the difference between right and left without yelling at him, but I was unsuccessful.

I had no personal experience with the Drum and Bugle Corps, but I believe that it was the most challenging company to lead, or, for that matter, to be in, as those in that company had to spend time practicing their instruments, in addition to drilling. Someone who had been in the Drum and Bugle Corps contends that holding a certain rank in the D & B Corps was the equivalent of holding a rank one level higher in another company; for example, a PFC in the D & B Corps would be the equivalent of being a corporal in another company, but I disagree.

Company Commanders would generally rise to the rank of Captain, although some graduated with the rank of First Lieutenant, sometimes not having been promoted to Captain, but more often having previously reached the rank of Captain but been demoted by one level for disciplinary reasons.

Each company consisted of two platoons. Neither the Company Commander nor the Company Sergeant belonged to either platoon.

The platoons were called First and Second Platoon, but despite the name implying that First was better or more prestigious, I think most will agree with me that the Second Platoon leader had a more challenging job at drill. As the First Platoon marched in front of the second, the Second Platoon leader found it more difficult to hear and repeat the Company Commander's commands, and had to get the timing just right when saying the second part of the command, as in "Reverse ... March!" Also, in the specific case of "Reverse ... March!" as soon as the command was given, the Company Commander ended up at the back of the marching platoon, with the leader of the Second Platoon leading the company until the Company Commander could make his way to what was now the front of the company. Outside of drill, the responsibility and challenge of leading the first or second platoon was the same. The Commandant had once mentioned that he did his best to balance the distribution of cadets who were either disciplinary problems, or especially good or bad at drill, both between the two platoons within a company and between the two junior and the two senior platoons. In his office he had a wall rack with a card for each cadet, arranged to show who was in which platoon and company, and what rank and position he held. The Commandant mentioned that many times he had taken an instant picture with a Polaroid camera, to study the composition of the Cadet Corps at home in the evening. (That was the state of available technology at the time.) He deserves credit for that.

Some Platoon Leaders had risen to First Lieutenant at the end of the year; others either had not been promoted to that rank, or had been promoted and then demoted, and graduated as Second Lieutenants. A few who had been bumped to private and had not had their rank restored still retained their position, often because it would not have been fair to those under their command to be assigned a new officer shortly before the Military Day drill competitions; they ended up being listed in the Military Day program as "Platoon Leader ... John Doe ... First Platoon Leader" instead of the typical "First Lieutenant ... John Doe ... First Platoon Leader." What may have looked like a mistake in the program to many parents and guests was painfully clear to those in the know.

I won't repeat my description of officer insignia, as I've

previously covered the topic in the first volume.

The Commandant was once asked why the insignia was different than the insignia used in the U.S. Military. His explanation (I'm paraphrasing) was that it was "Because if you're sitting in some shopping mall and some serviceman who's just come back from Vietnam sees you wearing officer insignia, he has to salute you." When someone said that he could obviously see that we were kids and not real officers, he said that it didn't matter; if he sees the insignia, he is required to salute you.

More so than other chapters, this chapter reflects my thoughts on the matter. Others will disagree with some of my views about the responsibility and desirability of the various positions.

13
Sister Mary David, O.S.B

Sister Mary David, who for many years (at least 1965-1973, possibly longer) was the principal of Linton Hall Military School, died on May 21, 2023. She was 93 years old.

Born Doris Carolyn Nolte on October 27, 1929 in Henrico, Virginia, just outside Richmond, she was one of seven children: four boys and three girls. Both her paternal grandparents were born in Germany; her maternal grandparents and her parents were all born in Virginia, according to U.S. Census records. Her oldest brother, William J. Nolte, Jr., became a Catholic priest; he died in 2002.

Doris Nolte entered the Benedictine sisters convent upon graduating from St. Gertrude High School in Richmond, and professed her vows in 1949, taking the religious name of Sister Mary David, presumably chosen from the names of two of her siblings.
She graduated from St. Joseph's College in Emmitsburg, Maryland and St. John's University in Collegeville, Minnesota.

She was principal of Linton Hall Military School in Bristow, Virginia for several years, where she also taught Mathematics and Science, and has also taught at other schools in Virginia. She subsequently received a nursing degree and specialized in care of the elderly and hospice care. In recent years she also participated in the BEACON adult literacy program.

She resumed use of her birth name, being known in later years as Sister Doris Nolte, OSB.

14
LHMS Videos on Youtube.com

The following are videos of Linton Hall Military School found on youtube.com.

Most videos were originally filmed with 8 mm or Super 8 film cameras, and transferred to video. The quality is not as good as it would be with today's technology, but we are fortunate that these videos were made, preserved and then shared for us to see. I am very grateful to all those who shared these.

I have included shortened urls, tiny.cc/LHMSvid1 through tiny.cc/LHMSvid14 to make it easier for you to type in your browser's search box.

https://www.youtube.com/shorts/yMo1koTD598
tiny.cc/LHMSvid1
Pans 360 degrees from the front of the school building, blacktop, convent, trees, back to building. Around 2012. Extraneous background sound of wind, passing cars. By rwvirginia.

https://www.youtube.com/watch?v=e2l1_jOgpzs
tiny.cc/LHMSvid2
Pans around the back of the building, blacktop, windbreak, canteen. Late 1970s. Some audio comments (turn up the volume.)
By Vince Wilding

https://www.youtube.com/watch?v=UTvnDETHO1E
tiny.cc/LHMSvid3
The first minute shows JFK's grave at Arlington National Cemetery. LHMS 1967-1970 begins at 1:10. Then there is marching at Linton Hall with cadets wearing sweaters and officers wearing helmets. Military Day begins at 3:15 including video of outdoor Mass. Apparently more than one Military Day is shown. Assorted music.
By KarnEvil4

https://www.youtube.com/watch?v=IkHqC7nxPKE
tiny.cc/LHMSvid4
Military Day, May 31, 1981. Looks a lot like Military Day a decade before. Military music medley at the beginning, background sounds of visitors talking. By Javier Regalado.

https://www.youtube.com/watch?v=UXWyiXQ8tE4
tiny.cc/LHMSvid5
Linton Hall School in Bristow, Virginia as it looks today (ca. 2021) with some buildings as I remember them, other new features such as the teaching garden. Video taken from a bike, Linton Hall starts at 3:16. Aerial drone views start at 6:43 with neglected/abandoned agricultural buildings and suburban sprawl near Linton Hall. At 8:43 biker leaves Linton Hall. Most of the video has been speeded up; you'll have to keep clicking on the pause button. Audio is background music.
By Christopher Brown.

The following were uploaded by Marianne Carney, and were taken in 1975-1976. Military Day and graduation had not changed much since the late 1960s when I attended, so these videos will be of interest to many LHMS alumni from earlier years.

https://www.youtube.com/watch?v=2E5wOkcdO_o
tiny.cc/LHMSvid6
Military Day on the blacktop, which happened when the parade field had been soaked by rain. Dormitory with messy beds and family members on the last day of the school year. Parade outside LHMS (unknown location.) No audio. May 1975. By Marianne Carney

https://www.youtube.com/watch?v=Iaz4-yUnKRs
tiny.cc/LHMSvid7
May 25, 1975 Military Day Mass indoors in gym; Military Day marching. No audio. By Marianne Carney.

https://www.youtube.com/watch?v=MX0_tYvDKYo
tiny.cc/LHMSvid8
Drum and Bugle Corps at parade in Culpeper, Va. May 1975.
No audio. By Marianne Carney

https://www.youtube.com/watch?v=siWqILoJj08
tiny.cc/LHMSvid9
May 1975 Drum and Bugle Corps parade in Manassas, Va. No audio.
By Marianne Carney.

https://www.youtube.com/watch?v=iuV61_uVH8U
tiny.cc/LHMSvid10
April 1975 Drum and Bugle Corps Retreat Parade, apparently includes Military Day footage. Home video after 2:34. No audio.
By Marianne Carney.

https://www.youtube.com/watch?v=Xn3BQugSvwg
tiny.cc/LHMSvid11
April 1975. LHMS starts at 0:23 after home video. No audio.
By Marianne Carney.

https://www.youtube.com/watch?v=icv6tTEVCN8
tiny.cc/LHMSvid12
May 1975 Military Day Awards. No audio. By Marianne Carney.

https://www.youtube.com/watch?v=DoMnt4eM5u4
tiny.cc/LHMSvid13
June 1, 1975 Linton Hall graduation in the gym; good closeups of graduating class posing outside the building starting at 1:55.
No audio. By Marianne Carney.

https://www.youtube.com/watch?v=h5xe1bAa244
tiny.cc/LHMSvid14
May 30, 1976 Military Day. No audio. By Marianne Carney

15
Military Day, 1948

Linton Hall's seventeenth Military Day took place on May 23, 1948. Mass celebrants were:
      Fr. Charles O'Laughlin, O.S.B. — Celebrant
      Fr. Vincent Sheppard, O.S.B. — Deacon
      Fr. Gregory Stevens, O.S.B. — Sub-Deacon
      Fr. Vito F. Cannizzo, C.P.S. — Master of Ceremonies
      Fr. Bernard Patterson, O.S.B. — Delivered the sermon

Commandant was Lt. Marlin S. Reichley

Cadet officers were:
        Lt. Col. James Craddock — Battalion Commander
        Major James Welch — Adjutant

Company A
        John Kirchmier — Captain
        Arthur Pettipas — First Lieutenant
        Jes Quisenberry — Second Lieutenant

Company B
        Tommy Follin — Captain
        Robert Rasmussen — First Lieutenant
        Edward Barnette — Second Lieutenant

Company C
        Milton Speroni — Captain
        Jack McDonald — First Lieutenant
        Patrick Cinnamond — Second Lieutenant

Company D
        Jose Aranda — Captain
        Ray Morales — First Lieutenant
        Bill Balser — Second Lieutenant

Company E
        Jack Joyce — Captain
        Michael Fox — First Lieutenant
        Earl Froman — Second Lieutenant

Drum and Bugle Corps
        Jerry Frazier — Captain

16
Military Day Address, 1950

Below is a transcript of the address by Fr. Walter W. Herbert, of St. Mary's Church in Alexandria, Virginia, on the Nineteenth Annual Military Day (1950.)[21] A beautiful speech, although it ignores the fact that not all memories of Linton Hall may have been pleasant.

A school is like a great tree which grows from a tiny seed planted in the depths of the earth. Each year, it puts forth leaves, and then, when they are mature, sends them out on the wings of the wind to all parts of the earth. And each one of these leaves bears unmistakably the mark of the tree from which it came.

Fifty-six years ago, a seed was planted in this green valley. Now, it has grown and become a great school which each year sends forth its students, each bearing the mark of the things he has learned here.

Out from this valley they go, one by one, that they may be lights to light up the darkness of our times. They go out that by the teachings of our Lord, they may be guides to lead in a world in which leadership has come to mean the same as force.

The challenge which the world throws into the face of you who go out from this school is not an easy one. Here in classroom and chapel, you have learned of the gentle Christ and have been taught that you should obey Him. But if you try to be good, the only thing the world will say is that you are weak. Here you have been taught of the goodness of God, and yet if you believe in God, the only thing that men may say about you is that you are old-fashioned. Here you have been taught that your soul is more important than anything else in the world, but if you value your self-respect more than the opinions of others, the only thing that they may say about you is that you are foolish. They said the same things about our Blessed Lord in his day, and He knew that nearly 2,000 years later they would be making the same remarks about His followers,

---

[21] *Congressional Record* April 21-June 07, 1950: Vol 96 Appendix page A4162

and that is why He could declare from another mountain to those sitting in another green valley:

"Blessed are ye when they shall revile you and persecute you and speak all that is evil against you untruly for my sake, for your reward is very great in Heaven." (Matthew v: 11-12.)

And that is why also, in the Sacrament of Confirmation, He sent you the Holy Ghost, to make you strong and perfect Christians and soldiers of the King.

But as you go out into the fight for Christ, we would that you be not merely fighters in the ranks, but leaders. We wish that your good example may shine before all that many may be moved to draw close to God because of you. It is a strange thing but true that a soul which turns its back upon God is not satisfied to go along its own miserable way to destruction alone, but must draw others after. But if that is true, it is equally true that if a soul loves God it cannot rest until all around it love God also. That is why saints are so unpopular and disturbing to many in the world. That is why they are thought to be weak, old-fashioned, or foolish. That is the challenge that you have to face. This is the challenge for which you have been preparing these many years at Linton Hall.

You will take many memories with you as you leave these grounds in a few short weeks. There will be memories of friends, of good times spent, of games won, of the give and take of school life, which is only a little preview of the give and take of your life outside. As the years go on and these things become dim in your memories, you will forget much of what has happened. But there is one thing about Linton Hall that few of you will ever be able to forget, and that is the sacrifice and devotion to those who labor here. Fifty-six years ago, four nuns planted the seed that is today Linton Hall. The struggles that have intervened have not been easy. There have been dark days when all seemed lost, days of hardship and poverty, but in spite of all this, Linton Hall prospered, for it is like the house in Scripture: "The rains descended and the floods came, and the winds blew and dashed against that house and it fell not, because it was founded upon a rock." (Matthew vii: 25.)

Those four brave souls have now become 84, and the original handful of students become 247. And now a new hall must be added to shelter the ever-growing number of those who come. Indeed, these stones must rise and continue to rise in the years to come as a glowing tribute to the dreams of those who first planted the seed, and as a pledge that all those who have labored here have not labored in vain.

May nothing that you ever do betray the trust that those who have been your teachers place in you as you go forth. May nothing that you ever do erase the mark which Linton Hall places upon you, for it is the mark of the cross of our Lord.

May you keep your faith, may you love all men. If you do, then in the words of St. Paul: "I am sure that neither death nor life, nor angels nor principalities, nor powers, nor things present, nor things to come, nor might, nor height, nor depth, nor any other creature shall be able to separate you from the love of God which is in Christ Jesus our Lord." (Romans viii: 38-39.)

Below: Topographic map, 1968 edition, as used in Military Science class. Linton Hall Military School is at the bottom of the map.

17
Lt. Lawrence Scott Carson, Jr., Linton Hall's Second Commandant

Linton Hall Military School's second Commandant, from 1932 through 1935, was 1st Lt. Scott Carson, Jr., Cavalry Reserves, U.S. Army.

Born at Ft. Leavenworth, Kansas on February 4, 1904,[22] he attended Porter Military Academy in Charleston, South Carolina and subsequently graduated from the United States Military Academy, Virginia Military Institute with a Bachelor of Science Degree. He later studied Physics and Engineering at the University of Tennessee at Chattanooga.

On Feb. 6, 1928, just two days after his twenty-fourth birthday, he was commissioned Second Lieutenant in the Organized Reserves and was assigned to the 306th Cavalry Regiment, 62nd Cavalry Division in Washington, D.C. as a First Lieutenant.

From 1932-1935 he was the Commandant at LHMS.

On May 1, 1935 he was ordered to active duty with the C.C.C. at Fort Meade, and later to the Wolf Rock Camp at Philipsburg, Pennsylvania, then to Damascus with the 357th Company.

On July 30, 1944 he was discharged from the Army.

He died on November 10, 1947 at age 43, and is buried at Arlington National Cemetery, Section 1, Lot 889. A Protestant chaplain was requested at his interment.

---

[22] *Backbone Star,* Dec. 15, 1935, p. 4-5; *Washington Evening Star*

REGISTRATION CARD—(Men born on or after February 17, 1897 and on or before December 31, 1921)

SERIAL NUMBER: T 3130
1. NAME (Print): LAWRENCE Scott CARSON
ORDER NUMBER: T 11643A

2. PLACE OF RESIDENCE (Print): 3107 Homewood Ave - Balto Md
[THE PLACE OF RESIDENCE GIVEN ON THE LINE ABOVE WILL DETERMINE LOCAL BOARD JURISDICTION; LINE 2 OF REGISTRATION CERTIFICATE WILL BE IDENTICAL]

3. MAILING ADDRESS: Same

4. TELEPHONE:
5. AGE IN YEARS: 40
DATE OF BIRTH: Feb 4 1904
6. PLACE OF BIRTH: Fort Leavenworth, Kansas

7. NAME AND ADDRESS OF PERSON WHO WILL ALWAYS KNOW YOUR ADDRESS: Mrs Frances N. Carson - 2112-O St. N.W. Washington D.C.

8. EMPLOYER'S NAME AND ADDRESS: Md State Health Dept-2

9. PLACE OF EMPLOYMENT OR BUSINESS: 2411 N. Charles St - Balto Md.

I AFFIRM THAT I HAVE VERIFIED ABOVE ANSWERS AND THAT THEY ARE TRUE.

Lawrence S. Carson
(Registrant's signature)

D. S. S. Form 1
(Revised 1-1-42)

18
"Whatever I was doing, I was doing it for God because He wanted me to do it."
– Sister Mary David, O.S.B

Just four months after I corresponded with Sister Mary David, as reported in Chapter 8, "Sister Mary David Writes Back," she was quoted in the *Catholic Herald*[23] as saying the above words on the occasion of her seventieth anniversary as a nun.

  Everything? Really?

  I don't want to discount the possibility that she was misquoted, or that she unintentionally misspoke. For her sake, I hope that's the case, but given her reply which I quoted in Chapter 8, I doubt it.

  She did much good and also did much harm. As Principal she had the ultimate power to make Linton Hall live up to its full potential and be a wonderful school, but it was far from it.

---

[23] "Bishop Burbidge Celebrates Mass for Religious Sister Jubilarians" *Catholic Herald,* February 2, 2019.

19
Photos

The following four postcards depict the Linton Hall Guest House. The building was originally St. Anne's Convent, built in 1897. It was converted to a guest house in 1915, and the building was demolished in 1978.

44

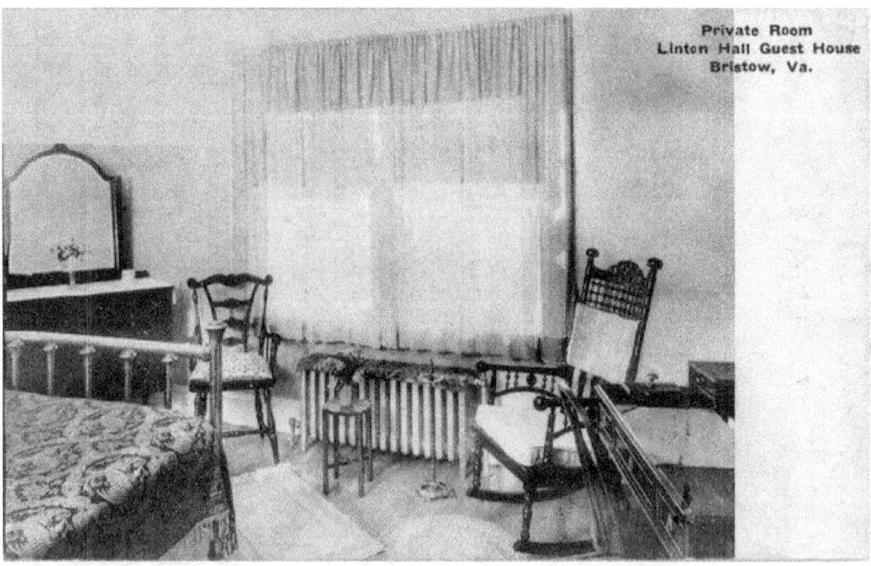

Private Room
Linton Hall Guest House
Bristow, Va.

Above: The original LHMS Building

Below: Linton Hall Military School Band, ca. 1941

20
Bill Farquhar, Gym Teacher and Coach

William Francis Farquhar, "Bill," was born on September 30, 1915 in Washington D.C., and was a Linton Hall Military School alumnus. He subsequently attended and graduated from Gonzaga High School in Washington, D.C.. He began teaching and coaching at Linton Hall Military School in 1940.

On November 12, 1941 he enlisted in the U.S. Army and served during World War II and was discharged on May 15, 1945 with the rank of Private.

He returned to Linton Hall where he was coach and gym teacher, more recently with the title of Athletic Director, for the rest of his life.

On Dec. 27, 1949 he married Margaret Virginia, and they would later have one daughter.

Bill died on January 4, 2011 at the age of 95.

His wife, Margaret Virginia Farquhar was born on November 3, 1910 and died on March 16, 1979 at age 68.

Mr. and Mrs. Farquhar are both buried in the Linton Hall cemetery.

The Linton Hall school gym was renamed the William Farquhar Sports Center in his memory.

21
More About Linton Hall Alumnus
John Phillips of The Mamas and the Papas

In Chapters 34 and 35 of the first volume, I wrote about what LHMS alumnus John Phillips of The Mamas and the Papas said about Linton Hall in his autobiography, *Papa John.*[24] Here are a few more interesting facts.

• John's adoptive father was Marine Corps Captain Claude Andrew Phillips. His biological father was Roland Meeks, a doctor in the Marines, who died in a Japanese Prisoner of War camp before John was born.

• At Linton Hall, John rose to at least the rank of Corporal. An undated photo in his book shows him in the LHMS uniform with Corporal stripes and two ribbons.

• His musical talent manifested itself early; he was named best boy in the Linton Hall school band trumpet solos.

• His full name was John Edmund Andrew Phillips.

• He recalls "penguins [nuns] watched us shower and hit us… who wants [l]imits after four years of that?" He subsequently refers to leaving Linton Hall by saying his "sentence had been commuted" and states that the "paddle whomping nuns … may have instilled a hatred of authority and regimentation" in him.

• In spite of earning bad grades at The Bullis School, an all-boys boarding school, he was awarded an appointment to the Naval Academy in Annapolis, Maryland, which — not surprisingly — he disliked and described as "Linton Hall for adults." He tried to get out by

---

[24] Phillips, John: *Papa John – An Autobiography.* New York: Doubleday & Co., 1986 (hardcover.) Also published in paperback by Dell in 1987

accumulating demerits, and had reached 297 of the required 300 demerits when, on the occasion of Queen Elizabeth's visit in November 1954, his demerits were forgiven. According to his book, any visiting royalty or head of state had the power to grant amnesty on all demerits – and she did.

His next attempt to get kicked out of Annapolis was to fake blind spots which were purportedly the result of him having been dropped on his head at age 3 (which really did happen) and he was given a medical discharge in March, 1955.

22
Linton Hall During the Mid-1970s

During the mid-1970s, Linton Hall's enrollment was declining. I believe that this was due both to the Vietnam war making anything having to do with the military unpopular, and to the harsh punishments that were used at Linton Hall.

The school dropped the word *military* from its name, but other than that, the daily schedule was the same, the uniforms the same, the military program the same, according to a school brochure from 1978 and what I observed when I re-visited Linton Hall on Military Day 1980. The Commandant was still there, Bill was still there, but the principal was now Sister Mary Ellen. Most of the nuns who taught or were dormitory prefects were new to me, and about three quarters of them no longer wore the habit.

In addition to dropping the word *military* from its name, the school tried hard to change its image by de-emphasizing, or even concealing, the military aspect. An article about Linton Hall in the *Potomac News* (a low-circulation local newspaper) dated May 5, 1975 states that "The [C]ommandant explained that the military aspect of the school has nothing to do with guns or the armed forces. The cadets do drill in military fashion; the [C]ommandant explained that the purpose of the drills is to improve motor skills."[25] Sister Christine was quoted in the same article as saying that the program "isn't regimented." These are two egregious examples of the many ways Linton Hall misrepresented itself.

The declining enrollment caused a serious financial problem, since most of the costs (maintenance and repair of the building and other facilities, heating and lighting, and staff salaries to name the major ones) stayed the same. The variable costs, i.e. costs that varied depending on the number of cadets were small in comparison (primarily food, laundry and uniforms; the fact that the cost of uniforms was billed separately is irrelevant.) In order to spread the fixed costs among fewer students the school would have had to dramatically raise tuition, and the higher

---

[25] "We've Found a Happy Medium: Linton Hall Military School Guides Boys Along Christian Principles" *Potomac News,* May 5, 1975

tuition would have caused enrollment to decrease even further, thus creating a vicious cycle.

Linton Hall placed newspaper ads to try to increase enrollment. In addition to advertising in the *Washington Post,* it cast a wider net by advertising in newspapers in Richmond, Va. and Greensboro, N.C..

Left: *Richmond Times-Dispatch,* May 9, 1971. Right: *Greensboro* (North Carolina) *Daily News,* March 11, 1973.

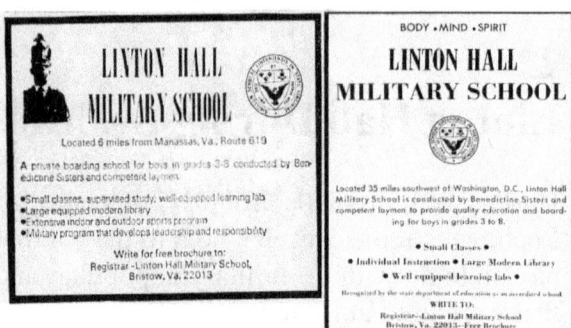

Another change is that on Sunday, February 17, 1974, Linton Hall Military School held a buffet dinner and dance for cadets, their parents and friends to celebrate Valentine's Day.[26] I've seen a photo of a dance at Linton Hall in which girls the cadets' age were present, so I'm pretty sure the cadets didn't dance with each other or with the nuns. During the years I attended Linton Hall, a school dance would have been unthinkable.

Cadets were also permitted to have longer hair, the length that was common among boys outside of Linton Hall during the late 1960s. (Faces covered for privacy.)

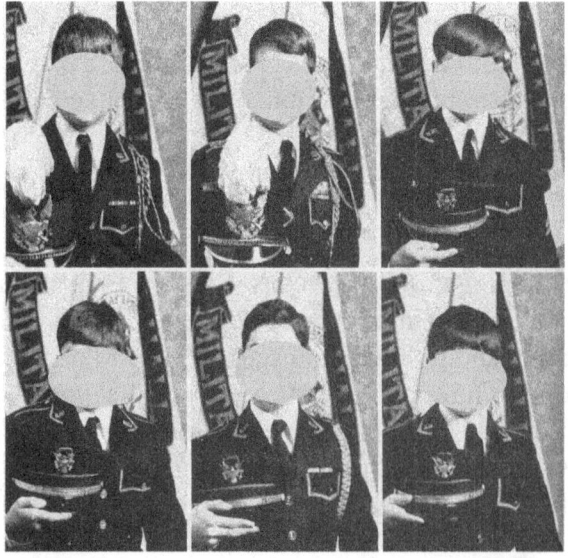

---

[26] "Valentine Dance" *Potomac News,* February 22, 1974

23
Father Blase Strittmatter, O.S.B.

When I attended Linton Hall Military School, Father Blase Raymond Strittmatter, O.S.B., was the school and convent chaplain. (His first name was misspelled as Blaise in the school yearbook.)

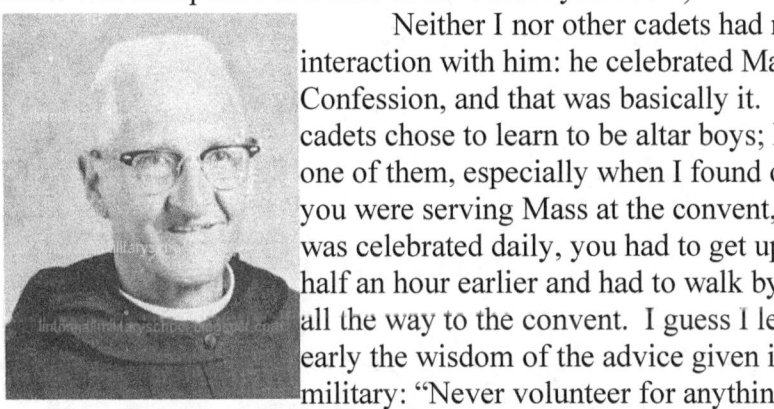

Neither I nor other cadets had much interaction with him: he celebrated Mass, heard Confession, and that was basically it. Some cadets chose to learn to be altar boys; I was not one of them, especially when I found out that if you were serving Mass at the convent, where it was celebrated daily, you had to get up about half an hour earlier and had to walk by yourself all the way to the convent. I guess I learned early the wisdom of the advice given in the military: "Never volunteer for anything."

Those who were serving Mass would tie the belt from their bathrobe to the frame of their bed, so that the dormitory prefect could find their bed in the dark in order to wake them up half an hour or so before all the others – which also meant that the nun herself had to get up earlier, since she never left her room without wearing her full habit; not once in all my years there did I see a nun wearing a bathrobe, or even slippers.

Since Fr. Blase did not have any disciplinary responsibilities, I did not fear him. He did have the habit of calling everyone Charlie, regardless of his name, which some saw as an amusing eccentricity, and which I saw as demeaning in the same way that once upon a time white customers would call black porters George.

Now on to his biography …

Blase Strittmatter was born on June 21, 1905 in Carroltown, Pa., a small town in central Pennsylvania's coal mining country and which today has fewer than 900 inhabitants. His father Edward was a blacksmith, his mother's name was Rose and he had at least one brother and two sisters; one of his sisters became a nun. He attended St. Vincent Prep and College in Pennsylvania, and also studied at St. Anselm College in Rome, Italy.

On July 2, 1926, just a few days after his twenty-first birthday, he became a Benedictine monk. Five years later, on June 28, 1931 he became a Catholic priest. He subsequently joined the faculty at St. Vincent College and Seminary, where he taught Philosophy.

Fr. Blase lived most of his life at St. Vincent Abbey in Latrobe, Pa., which is just east of Pittsburgh. He was also Associate Pastor in the Archdiocese of Chicago and the Diocese of Greensburg.

On October 16, 1940, when he was 35 years old and World War II had just started, he registered for the draft, listing his height as 5'9" and his weight at 185 pounds. I was unable to find out whether or not he was drafted. I doubt it, since I vaguely recall that in the 1970s, during the Vietnam war, religious ministers received either an automatic deferment or exemption, although they were required to register for the draft just like any other man.

For several years he was chaplain to the sisters at Bristow, Va. and the students at Linton Hall. In 1984 he returned to St. Vincent Abbey. Father Blase died of a heart attack on June 18, 1986, just three days before what would have been his 81st birthday. He is buried at St. Vincent Cemetery.

24
Punishments

Linton Hall's cadets ranged from age seven to as old as fifteen, possibly even sixteen years old. Seven years is the generally accepted "age of reason" at which a child is considered to have reached a sufficient level of maturity to understand the difference between right and wrong, and who can understand explanations as to why he should, or should not, perform certain actions. The reasons why he should not play with matches, get in a car with strangers, or why he should brush his teeth or do his homework can be explained in simple terms so that he understands the consequences of certain actions and inactions. Children will often forget and have to be reminded. Other children may be impulsive and not consider the consequences of their actions; and others may be rebellious for a host of reasons.

My point is that a simple explanation should be the first, and often the second and third option before punishment should be resorted to and, even then, punishment should be in proportion to the transgression.

I've given examples of reasonable expectations such as "don't play with matches" and "brush your teeth."

But expectations can be unreasonable, too. Children like to play, laugh, run, joke and explore the world around them (which has a newness which most of those reading these words have long ago stopped experiencing.) All this is natural and normal. It is totally unreasonable to expect a child, or an adult for that matter, to stand still for minutes at a time, not even speaking (words such as unconscious, catatonic, sedated, stoned and overmedicated with tranquilizers come to mind.) Nor is it reasonable to expect anyone with half a brain, child or adult, to thrive, learn and grow mentally, emotionally and spiritually when treated as an automaton in a highly regimented, restrictive environment where there is no opportunity for personal autonomy and decision making.

Yet that is exactly what was expected of us at Linton Hall. Great preparation for life in a monastery, the military, prison or an insane asylum, but not for becoming an autonomous adult with initiative, drive, the ability to discern right and wrong, the willingness to learn and face new challenges, and to use his talents in a positive and productive way. Isn't this what the Parable of the Talents (Matthew 25:14-30) is all about?

This was a long introduction to the subject of this chapter — punishment. I contend that the punishments that were meted out as a result of breaking a rule, whether intentionally or by error (as we, imperfect beings, are bound to do) were disproportionately harsh and cruel, yet all too common. I believe that any good, reasonable person who is not a sadist will agree with me.

Standing at attention

This required standing still, arms hanging down, without moving for an extended period of time, typically anywhere from ten minutes to an hour or longer. Even the slightest movement would often result in the time being extended. This may seem like no big deal if you try it for a few seconds, but it soon becomes unbearable as the need to scratch your nose or shift your weight from one foot to the other becomes greater and greater. It's even worse when you aren't facing a clock and have no idea how much time has elapsed and how much time remains. Typically any clock would be behind you, as the officer would position you so as to have both you and the clock in his view. Sounds bad, but this was probably the mildest punishment.

It could be worse, however, if you needed to urinate (and lacking the freedom to do so makes the need feel more intense.) It was also bad if this punishment happened at mealtime, when you had to watch others eat and were finally told to sit down just as the time for the meal was almost over, so you had to wolf down what was on the tray as quickly as possible. If made to stand at attention during a movie, you would have to do so with your back to the screen, but since you would have to stand in a place out of the way of the others who were seated as they watched the movie, it was difficult for the officer to notice if you occasionally turned your head.

A variation used by at least one officer was to have the cadet stand with his back to the lockers in the dorm. The officer would make a movement as to punch you, but at the very last instant his hand would strike the locker next to you, with his palm open. The locker would make a frightening sound, and there was no way to know whether the next time he would hit the locker again, or hit you.

This punishment was something only an officer would do, as officers were not allowed to strike cadets, and this rule was either never or extremely rarely broken.

But officers had another punishment in their arsenal.

Deep knee bends

A variation of the above, except that you would be in a deep squat, heels off the floor, torso vertical, with hands and arms not touching the floor, so they could not be used to support your weight or even help you maintain your balance. Although slight movement was typically not disallowed, this position causes intense pain as muscles and ligaments are pulled, and joints are strained. The longer this position is held, the stronger the pain becomes. Needless to say, in addition to causing pain, this causes damage to muscles, ligaments and joints (particularly the cartilage,) yet it leaves none of the visible marks that a beating would leave.

Some clever cadets claimed to be "double jointed," that is, that they had an extra bone in their joints which meant that they could not do deep knee bends. This almost always meant that the officer would have to use an alternate form of punishment, and since officers were not permitted to strike a cadet, the alternate form of punishment would be milder, as being made to stand at attention.

There was no way for the officer to verify whether the cadet in question had an extra bone in his joints or was lying, and the officer would typically give the cadet the benefit of the doubt.

By the way, being "double jointed" as described above is a myth. There is no such thing as having an extra bone at the joint. What is referred to as being "double jointed" is actually a misnomer; it involves the ligaments being longer than normal, so that the knee or elbow can be hyperextended, i.e., extended past 180 degrees.

I am ashamed that as an officer I did make cadets do deep knee bends. I also believed at the time that being double jointed was real, and fell for that trick. I was not privy to the trick, however, when I was the one being made to do deep knee bends my first year at Linton Hall.

The cross

Although the nuns, and less frequently the Commandant, used standing at attention as a punishment, there was one punishment which only the Commandant used. This variation of standing at attention involved standing with arms out horizontally, with each hand holding a rifle which was held vertically, a position similar to Jesus nailed to the cross, hence the name.

Holding this position for an extended amount of time becomes excruciatingly painful. If you allowed your arms to move slightly down from the horizontal, the Commandant, who would be standing behind you holding a third rifle, would use that rifle to hit you in the elbow to make you resume the horizontal position. As with deep knee bends, this punishment was painful yet showed no visible signs of injury, such as welts or bruises. This was a punishment that I never received.

The paddle

This was used only by the nuns. Each nun who was in charge of a dormitory, as well as the Principal, Sister Mary David, had one of her own. I don't recall whether nuns who taught in the classroom had one, but if not they could have borrowed one had they chosen to do so. This was a piece of wood about 18 inches long, 2 to 3 inches wide, and about half an inch thick. Understandably, I never had the opportunity to actually measure it. The recipient would be made to bend down at the waist and hold on to his ankles, and the sadistic nun would hit him to her cruel heart's content, typically on the upper part of the back of the leg rather than the buttocks, but given the ferocity with which this was done, you could be hit elsewhere as well. The number of paddlings would depend on the severity of the offense as well as the nun's level of anger.

In my years at Linton Hall I was only paddled on one occasion (I don't remember how many hits I received, but it was several) by an uncontrollably angry Sister Mary David herself, for something I did not do. She was someone who punished first, and only later possibly bothered to find out whether the punished cadet was guilty. The injustice of it was probably even worse than the physical pain. Injustice was common at Linton Hall.

A nun who frequently used the paddle was Sister Theresa Anderson, who was in charge of the dormitory of a junior company (i.e., younger cadets) and also taught second graders. During Mass, if she thought one of the little boys wasn't singing loudly enough, she would have him hold out his hands and hit his hands with her paddle. The cries of pain from those being hit were loud enough to be heard by everyone at Mass, not just those nearby who were in her company. This happened at every Mass, to several boys. I wonder whether the purpose of making her cadets sing louder was to mask the noise of the cries from those she had just hit? Ironically, one of the hymns we sang at Mass had the lyrics "Whatsoever you do to the least of my brothers, that you do unto me." which is a paraphrase of Matthew 25:35-40.

The strap

Unlike the nuns, the Commandant did not use a paddle, but instead used a leather strap, similar to a thick, wide leather belt. It was rare for him to use it, typically on someone who had run away, been caught and brought back. Those beatings were done in front of the entire Battalion, which had been assembled and made to watch. He probably thought that by making an example of a runaway he was dissuading the rest of us from doing so, and that was probably the case. At the same time, it greatly reduced the level of admiration I had for him, and replaced admiration with fear of him. The fact that he assembled the entire battalion to watch means that he thought he was doing nothing wrong and there was nothing to hide — and that is sad as well.

An employer who beat an adult employee that way would be arrested, convicted and sued for every penny he's got; and that's an employee who as an adult is better able to defend himself and can quit at any time. Anyone who beat a dog that way would be arrested and charged with animal cruelty. But when an adult man or woman beat a small child at Linton Hall, it was business as usual.

Since I began writing about LHMS, I've heard from a couple of hundred alumni. What's tragic is that some of those who were beaten see nothing wrong with it.

Urine-soaked pajamas

On occasion, a child will urinate in his sleep and wet the bed. This happens more often to very young children. The important fact is that it's completely involuntary. Yet anyone this happened to would be punished by being made to wear his urine-soaked pajama bottoms around his neck for the whole day. This punishment was meted out by either the officers or the dormitory prefect, but was unavoidably obvious to all the nuns, the Commandant and Bill. We all wore uniforms, so the pajamas around the neck could be spotted from a hundred feet away. I describe this more fully on pages 23 and 24 of the first volume, but it bears repeating. The real object was to cause humiliation and bullying. There must be a special place in Hell for those who did this.

Bullying and public humiliation

This was the real objective behind making bedwetters wear their urine-soaked pajamas around their neck.

In other cases, when a cadet was being punished by being made to stand at attention, or holding two rifles, there were some cadets who would whisper "Suffer" and/or make the hand gesture which had that meaning. I never saw that kind of schadenfreude in any other of the schools I attended.

Mass punishment

Whenever a rule was broken and the culprit or culprits could not be identified, the entire group was punished, whether it was an entire class of 30 or the entire battalion of 250 cadets. The thought behind it was, better to punish two hundred innocent cadets, than to let one guilty cadet go unpunished. That is the exact opposite of the principle of jurisprudence that holds that in a criminal trial, one must be convicted beyond a reasonable doubt, and that if there is doubt or insufficient evidence, the accused must not be convicted.

The mass punishment often was having to stand at attention without moving (including not being allowed to use the bathroom) for a prolonged amount of time, being made to march during what would have been free time or having to run in circles around the blacktop no matter how cold or hot it was, but other types of punishment were sometimes used.

The principle is not much different than when an army occupying a town announces that for each of its soldiers who is killed, ten civilians will be rounded up and shot, though clearly the consequences at Linton Hall were nowhere as dire.

To the credit of all of us who were subject to mass punishment over the years, I know of not a single instance in which someone who knew who the culprits were ratted them out.

Demerits

Both officers and nuns had the power to issue demerits. Typically these had to be worked off by marching during free time. The officers were assigned turns to direct the marching, so they/we officers also ended up losing some of our free time. The worst part about demerits was that if you accumulated a certain number (I believe it was three) you could not go home for the weekend until the number of outstanding demerits had been reduced below that number.

There was also a different type of demerit, called an academic demerit. I'm not quite sure how those worked, whether they affected your academic grade, or your grade for effort in that particular subject. I do know that unlike disciplinary demerits, a note would be sent to your parents informing them that you had received an academic demerit, because it happened to me. The reason? There was a teacher who would sometimes assign homework to be done during the weekend you went home. No other teacher did that, even on the alternate weekends when we stayed at Linton Hall, since there was no Study Hour on weekends. One assignment involved reading the articles in the Sunday paper about a particular major news event, and writing a report including pictures cut out from the newspaper. I did do that assignment, but it took a couple of hours out of the precious few hours I had at home. The next time she gave such an assignment I didn't do it, and that was what the demerit was for.

Court martials

Serious offenses could result in a court martial. This was somewhat like a trial, in which the officers acted as jurors. The accused had a brief opportunity to address the charges against him, and would then step outside while the officers discussed the matter. In practice it was the Commandant who "suggested" whether or not the cadet was guilty and what the appropriate punishment should be, and all the officers just happened to agree with what the Commandant said. No surprise there.

Other punishments

This list is far from complete. There was being made to chew a bar of soap for using offensive language, not being given the candy bar that was being distributed to everyone (there was an incentive for the nun doing the distribution to have an excuse to either eat it herself or use it as a reward to someone who did extra chores, such as sorting clean laundry) and not being allowed to go home for the weekend, among others. The last one I mentioned was a tacit acknowledgment that having to spend the weekend at Linton Hall was a punishment in itself.

I only missed a weekend home, not as punishment but because no one could come pick me up, for reasons that are not relevant. It was unpleasant and disappointing to miss out on family and the comforts and freedom of being home. However, it was not as bad as it seemed. Typically there would be very few of us there, with everyone except the Mexicans having gone home, and there was much less discipline or structure than there normally was.

What we were punished for

I suspect that the reason why running away from Linton Hall was considered such a major offense was not so much concern for the safety of the one running away, but the embarrassment that Linton Hall was such an awful place that cadets would willingly make the effort and take the risk of running away. After all, that was the reason that outgoing mail was censored — to keep parents from knowing the true conditions at Linton Hall. Before I was sent to Linton Hall I did spend a couple of summers at camp (not Camp Linton.) It would have been crazy to run away from such fun.

But the other infractions were quite minor: not singing loud enough at Mass, saying a "four letter word" within earshot of a nun, talking after lights out or while standing in line. One time when I was new I went to brush my teeth after being given the evening candy bar. An officer told me not to go; I went anyway and got enough demerits to miss a weekend home. I was extremely lucky that he either forgot to turn in the demerits, or had second thoughts, and I was able to go home.

There were also occasions in which cadets were punished for something that was not within their control. Wetting the bed is one example. Another was being late returning to Linton Hall from a weekend at home. It was completely up to the parents when to leave home and how much extra time to allow for traffic jams and other contingencies. Yet the sons were held liable for it. This rule was strictly enforced; even if you were just one minute late you would be given demerits which had to be marched off. In my years there I came back late just once, and by less than five minutes. My name ended up on the list posted on the Commandant's bulletin board, but for some reason (maybe because it was my first time returning late) I did not end up having to march off the demerit. As in much of what happened at Linton Hall, there was no explanation, just a pleasant surprise.

I'm firmly convinced that, in most cases, the only lasting effect of these punishments was make someone think of ways to not to get caught again, rather than to stop the disapproved behavior. That, plus anger and resentment.

What we were not punished for

Given the severity and disproportionality of punishments that were meted out for the above infractions, it still surprises me that other actions brought forth no more than being told to stop doing it.

Offensive and belittling language, when used by one cadet towards another, or by an officer towards a cadet is one example.

There was one cadet who owned a genuine Nazi helmet, which he would sometimes wear during recess, and he would walk around pretending to be a Nazi. Maybe at some point he was told to take the helmet home and not bring it back, but while he was acting like a Nazi no one told him not to do that or explained why. He was a seventh grader, so he was certainly old enough to understand the reasons.

Another cadet had the ability to roll his eyes upward so far that only the sclera (white part of the eye) would show. He would do that while pretending (I certainly hope he was pretending!) to worship the Devil during "rest" — the free period in the dorms. His behavior scared the living daylights out of many kids, and for good reason, yet nothing was done about it — by nuns, and in a Catholic school!

Not everyone was treated the same

To some extent, it's understandable that someone who normally followed the rules and made an innocent mistake would be treated less harshly than someone who had major disciplinary problems when both committed the same offense.

This benefited me starting my first year there, but much more so when I was in the eighth grade and was an officer.

I can remember two occasions when, as an officer, I openly defied the instructions of the prefect of my dorm. The first was over something minor, which could even be considered as doing something differently instead of defiance, but the second was a clear-cut case of defiance. In both cases, all she did was say "I don't appreciate what you did," and that was the end of the matter. I may not even have apologized. The reason I was able to get away with it must have been that I was effective in controlling the cadets under my command, and saved her from dealing with all the problematic behavior that might have happened.

On both occasions I didn't know that her response would be so mild, and didn't even take a moment to consider that; in both cases I had acted on the spur of the moment.

The Commandant acted similarly. As I mentioned in Chapter 41 of the first volume, "The Things We Got Away With."

Lack of supervision
During free time, there was only one nun to supervise over 200 cadets. The nuns would typically spend time chatting with a group of cadets, as in the photo above, taken while I was attending LHMS. From this position a nun could not see behind the arsenal, windbreak or canteen, nor the bathroom in the basement of the building, where anything could happen without her knowledge, and she would only intervene if someone ran to her to tell her abut it.

It's not just Linton Hall
While I was at Linton Hall, I thought that LHMS was the exception, that no other school was as bad, as the three schools I had previously attended had been wonderful.

Unfortunately, that's not the case. These punishments were and are so widespread among so many schools, as well as foster homes and group homes, that simply entering a combination of two or more words such as *abuse, nuns, priests, boarding school, foster care* in a search engine will bring a large number of examples. It's almost as if those in charge of these places were reading from the same manual. As bad as Linton Hall was, many places are far worse.

I have to seriously wonder whether those who treated children that way really believe in God, Judgement Day and the hereafter.

25
School and Teachers

One of the first things I wrote about Linton Hall was that "Academics were generally good." That was because I went to a good school both before and after Linton Hall, and I experienced a smooth transition both entering and leaving Linton Hall; each grade was a bit more difficult than the previous, as I expected, but there was no marked contrast. That's the reason I didn't write much about my classroom experience.

I recently looked at my eighth grade report card and noticed that there were two grades for each subject. The first, for achievement, ranged up to 100 (though in practice 75 seems to have been the lowest possible grade; anyway that's the lowest grade I ever got.) The second number was for effort, where 1 was "best effort sustained," 2 was "average effort," and 3 was "little apparent effort."

The evaluation for effort seems totally subjective to me, and based on little more than guesswork, except in the most egregious cases. Also, there was one subject in which I had a grade of 95% in one quarter, and 96% in each of the other three quarters, yet I was graded 2 (average effort) for each of the four quarters. Does that mean that if I had put in more effort I would have gotten a perfect 100%? Or that I was able to get 96% without really trying?

Some people are just better at some subjects than others. For example, I've always done well in Math, not because I found it particularly enjoyable, but because I'm just naturally good with numerical calculations. I'm not good at memorizing little details (such as dates and places in History) so my grades were not as good in History, in spite of putting in a lot of effort, yet I was given a 3 (little apparent effort) when in fact I had to made a lot of effort in order to get a grade in the high eighties (equivalent to B+.)

Also, teachers were unaware of the level of previous exposure to a subject; what may have appeared to be lack of effort on my part in Religion class simply meant that I had not gone to any Catholic schools before, and my exposure to Religion had been limited to whatever preparation was required for my First Communion and Confirmation.

The teachers also were probably unaware of the fact that those who were officers had to supervise study hour for the lower grades and had to deal with numerous interruptions while doing so, so we had to stay for second study hour in order to get our studying done, which I often did.

Not all subjects had grades for effort, and those that did quite often only had an evaluation of effort for the first or second quarter. Maybe our teachers gave up because evaluating effort was so difficult.

The Literature portion of English class was especially well taught. We had to read George Orwell's *Animal Farm,* and several thought-provoking short stories, such as "Flowers for Algernon" by Daniel Keyes.[27] Without spoiling the plot, I can say that this short story is about a mentally retarded man who becomes more intelligent. The story has a parallel with Linton Hall. Children are trusting, small in size, not yet fully intellectually developed, but in a few years they grow up into adults who are able to more fully understand how they were treated, able to tell the world about it, and are able to defend themselves if physically attacked with a paddle or leather strap.

The class called Art was really more of a crafts class, and appeared to be taught at the same level for all ages. For example, one of our projects involved gluing overlapping strips of colored crepe paper on a rock, and once the glue had dried writing words on the rock with a marker. It's something a second grader can do, but not a challenge for seventh and eighth graders. As an eighth grader I would have preferred if we had spent more time drawing, and some time being shown examples of great art, instead of having spent several weeks building one of those ready-to assemble plastic car models. It was a popular hobby among boys at the time, but clearly not art. This is another example of LHMS not living up to its potential, as it would have been relatively inexpensive to buy a few slides of art masterpieces.

You would expect that a nun who had made a lifetime commitment to join a convent would know a lot about Religion, but one year I found Religion class disappointing.

One thing the nun who taught the class said was that someone who sinned occasionally was like a warm cup of coffee. If the coffee's hot, it's good, if it's cold you send it back, but if it's lukewarm you drink it but aren't too happy with it. It's a parable that she made up, to explain that it's better to sin a lot and repent than sin a little and not repent, but she couldn't really explain to my satisfaction why it was better to sin and repent than not sin at all.

One time when I wrote an assignment there was a word that she misunderstood and thought that I had gravely insulted the church, and was even about to call Father Blase about it. The word was correctly

---

[27] Originally written as a short story, it was later expanded into a book by the same name, and later turned into movie called Charly. I have not seen the movie, but in my opinion the short story is more powerful than the book.

used and there was no insult, but I had to explain to her what the word meant.

One time she taught about "phrasees." Someone asked whether she meant phrases. No, not *phrases* with one *e,* but *phrasees,* with two *e*'s, she answered. (No, it wasn't the Pharisees either.) It was some concept that entailed writing a phrase that supposedly summarized an entire paragraph. This made no sense. When someone writes a paragraph it's because the entire paragraph contains information, not because the entire contents can be summarized in one very short sentence. I own an excellent, very large dictionary and there is no word such as *phrasees;* this was a neologism that she had just made up.

Another time she had us write about an encounter, which she defined as an occasion when someone had had a positive impact on one's life. Interesting topic, but only marginally relevant to Religion class. Maybe she liked the word *encounter* because at that time (the late 1960s) there were events such as encounter groups.

Our Religion book that year wasn't much better. It contained examples of situations to be discussed in class. One such situation involved a girl who answered the phone at home with "It's your dime, start talking." At the time I considered that as an issue of whether or not her parents would approve of her using such a humorous greeting to answer the phone, not as a question of morality or religion, and still believe that's the case.[28]

There was also a nun, not the one I refer to above, who told us that the nuns would sometimes hear the Devil roaming the hallways of the convent in the middle of the night, and dragging metal chains up and down the stone stairs. A scary story, but it well could have been the pipes used for heating making a metallic sound as they expanded and contracted. That was the sound we would hear in the dorms when the heat started to come on shortly before Reveille.

---

[28] Note to younger readers: There were no cell phones back then, only land lines. Using a public pay phone cost ten cents for a local call at the time. Also, Caller ID did not yet exist, so I understand her parents' concern that there was no way to know before answering whether the caller was a friend of the girl or the father's employer.

26
Memories, Updates and Thoughts

The following is a collection of memories, updates and thoughts since the first volume of *Linton Hall Memories* was published ten years ago.

• Correction: In my first book in Chapter 21, "History of Linton Hall," I wrote that Sarah Linton (later Sister Mary Baptista,) who donated a large amount of land for the purpose of building two schools, had become a Benedictine nun. That is incorrect. She entered the Order of The Visitation of Holy Mary, located in Georgetown, Washington, D.C.. Members of that order are referred to as Visitandines, and use the initials V.S.M. after their name, so she would be Sister Mary Baptista, V.S.M..

• I have since learned that Sarah Linton was born on January 4, 1822 and died on October 25, 1901, in Washington, D.C.. She was 79 years old. She is buried in the Georgetown Visitation Monastery Cemetery. The Visitation sisters run an all-girls school, Georgetown Visitation Preparatory School.

• According to the dictionary, although the word *monastery* could be used to refer to the place where either monks or nuns live, the words convent and nunnery are more specific and therefore preferable, as they refer to only nuns (or sisters.)

• Eduardo Facha García, the boy who died at Linton Hall, died at the end of August 1954, and was already ten years old. I had previously only reported the year of death in the post about him. I do not know the precise date of death or cause. Tragedy struck his family again on Christmas Day, 1955 when his brother José María died at only six days old of broncho-------- [illegible handwriting on the death certificate.]

- A 1957 article which listed government officials whose children were attending integrated schools said that one Secretary's child was attending LHMS. The article also said that "The Roman Catholic church in the Washington archdiocese follows a policy of integration in its schools."[29]

- As of 1987 there were 55 nuns at Bristow, half the number that were there in 1963. Leisure activities included playing cards and visiting friends and family on the weekend, and sisters had their own rooms, far different from the type of life nuns led in earlier decades. The nuns had stopped wearing the traditional habits, and Sister Joan Ann, who was at the school during the 1960s, was now even dressing as a clown to entertain children.[30]

- The latest (2023-2024) photo of the sisters on osbva.org shows only 24 nuns.

- The May 27, 1942 issue of *The Washington Post* includes a photo of Military Day inspection, with a 5-year old cadet, Bobby R., being inspected by an Army lieutenant. It was bad enough that there were 7-year-olds when I attended LHMS, but to send a five-year old there!

- A May 5, 1994 *Washington Post* article commemorates the 100th anniversary of the nuns' arrival, and mentions that the school now had 155 students, 56% of them Catholic, and only 40% of the teachers were nuns.

- The Linton Hall Military School band could be heard on WRC Radio for 15 minutes on May 20, 1933 and a few other times during the 1930s.

- On Saturday May 12, 1934 the LHMS Band played at the White House.

- Two possible runaways were reported in the *Washington Evening Star*. I am only publishing their first names in order to protect their privacy.
    Michael, age 7, of Washington, D.C. on Saturday Sep. 7, 1946. He would have had to return to Linton Hall the following day to begin his second year. As his mother had divorced and remarried, it was possible that he ran away to his father.
    John, age 13, was reported missing one or two days before March 7, 1936 (the date of the article) and was believed to be on his way to D.C., where he lived.

---

[29] *Miami News*, Sep. 29, 1957

[30] *Free Lance-Star*, Aug. 14, 1987.

• Mother Claudia Garvey, O.S.B., Prioress of St. Benedict Convent since 1922, died at Georgetown University Hospital on March 24, 1961. She was 71 years old.

• Oscar Dumont Pittman, Jr. was killed at Iwo Jima in July 1944. He was 18 years old. He had been a corporal in the Color Guard at Linton Hall Military School.

• Another alumnus who was at Linton Hall at approximately the same time I was (he was there longer) used to publish an excellent blog about LHMS, which he has since taken down. However, by going to archive.org and entering lhmscadet.wordpress.com in the search box, I found that the archived version dated 9/15/2011 is the most comprehensive collection of his posts.

• Charles Carreon, who went to LHMS from sixth through eighth grade and graduated in 1965 or 1966, wrote about a typical day in the life at Linton Hall. Although the link I mentioned in my first book no longer works, his article is available on archive.org. In the search box enter http://www.american-buddha.com/day.in.life.htm
The May 13, 2013 version (among others) has this article.

• I remember when I was in bed, sick with the flu, Sister Vincent, the school nurse would send up a medical corpsman, a cadet who had learned first aid, with my meals and to take my temperature. I remember that the meal included some cooked ground meat (loose, not formed into a patty) seasoned with rosemary which was quite good and I had never eaten at Linton Hall either before, or after. I assume it was a special meal; I don't remember what else there was on the tray. So I got room service.

When the Medical Corpsman took my temperature, he used a rectal thermometer. It's different than an oral thermometer in that the glass of the rectal thermometer is thicker. Rectal thermometers are typically used only on babies and preschool children, who could not reliably hold the thermometer under the tongue without possibly biting it and breaking it. I wonder how the medical corpsmen were taught to use it. The only way I can think of is that they practiced on each other, which makes me glad that I wasn't a medical corpsman. I also noticed that after he took out the thermometer, he cleaned it off on the inside of my pajamas. He could have used a piece of toilet tissue instead.

Being made to stay in bed the whole time got boring really fast, as I had absolutely nothing to read, listen to, or do. One of the things I wished for while at Linton Hall was some quiet time to myself, just to think. I ended up with too much of a good thing, and was happy when I was no longer bedridden.

• Others have incorrectly reported that Sylvester Stallone attended Linton Hall Military School. He did not. His brother Frank Stallone did attend, but only for a short period.

• Louis John(?) LeMoine, the well-liked alumnus known to us as "Louie" who returned to LHMS where he spent most of his life doing lawn maintenance and as night watchman, was born September 1 or 3, 1927 and died November 30, 2009. He was 82 years old. When he registered for the draft on September 4, 1945 he listed his height as 5'7" and weight as 154 lbs. One source lists his birthplace as Washington, D.C.; another reliable source lists it as "unknown." I have found little, and conflicting information about him.

• When I received my diploma, I was impressed that the lettering was engraved. It was only a few days ago that I noticed that only part of the diploma which would apply to eighth grade graduation was engraved; the school name and logo at the top were printed by offset, so that the printer could print diplomas for multiple schools. Also, my name was listed as "Cadet (Rank) (Name.)"

• If you are searching for a particular alumnus, and he happens to have a not-too common name, a good people finder site is truepeoplesearch.com. This site is better than the sites I mentioned in the first volume.

• One time when I had been at Linton Hall just a couple of weeks Sister Mary David called me to her office, introduced me to a new student who was entering LHMS after the school year had started, and told me to take him to the cafeteria and ask Sister Benedict, who was in charge of the kitchen, to give him lunch, since he hadn't eaten. She prepared something cold, possibly a bologna sandwich and cold vegetables (I don't remember exactly) with the usual milk carton. The kid tasted the food and told me that the only good thing was the milk. He generously asked me whether I wanted any of his food, and I declined.

• In Chapter 24 (Getting "Bumped" — the Officers' Rite of Passage) of the first volume I described how several officers lost their rank, and said that I was one of them. I'll elaborate. Another officer told Sister Mary David that I had done something, which in fact I had not. To put it less kindly, he lied about me. Sister Mary David immediately told me that I was bumped, with no attempt to elicit the true facts, no court martial, nothing. When I told my dorm prefect about this, she told me that over the summer when there was a meeting between the nuns and Commandant to decide on who would be an officer and what each officer's position would be, that it had been a tossup as to whether I or my accuser would get which of two positions.[31] As it turned out, I had gotten the more desirable of the two, i.e., the one involving greater responsibility. So it became clear to me that he had lied in order to get my position.

When I went to see Sister Mary David the next morning with my bars, officer cord, officer's helmet and sabre strap to return them, she told me that she hadn't said that I was bumped, but that *as far as she was concerned* I was bumped, and that she still had to discuss this with the Commandant.

I don't know exactly what happened, but I strongly suspect that the Commandant intervened on my behalf, and quite possibly my dormitory prefect (who was happy with the job I was doing and did not want me to be replaced) intervened as well. So I kept my position but not the rank, until it was restored a few weeks later; I don't remember how many.

- On page 27 of the first volume I wrote about a cadet who had gone on a hunger strike in order to get sick and have to leave Linton Hall, and how Bill had tried to shove a popsicle into the boy's mouth, so violently that I was afraid that Bill would break his teeth or, even worse, that the cadet would choke to death on the popsicle if it got jammed down his throat. "Bill" is William Farquhar, in whose memory the school gym was renamed. The cadet had later secretly climbed to the top of the water tower, and when he was discovered was ordered by the Commandant to climb down. I always assumed that he had hidden there in order to secretly watch those searching for him. I shudder to even consider the possibility that he could have considered suicide. Not surprisingly, he succeeded in getting out of Linton Hall, either because he was expelled or because his parents decided that if he went to such lengths to get out, they should get him out.

---

[31] According to a source familiar with the process, the Commandant would write up a list of cadets, listing each cadet's current rank and the suggested promotion. The list started with the highest rank and ended with PFCs. This list consisted of several pages, including blank ones at the end where all the sisters who worked at the school (prefects, teachers and others) would write their comments. The Commandant would review the comments, but ultimately he had the final say.

The same process was used for medals and awards. For the good conduct ribbon, the whole school roster was used; one "no" and you did not get the ribbon.

He had a relatively common name, so I have not been able to locate him in all these years. I've sent a flyer about my blog, book and Facebook account to the twenty or so people in the Washington D.C. metropolitan area with the same name, but have not heard from him. If he was one of those I wrote to, I completely understand his wish to not rekindle old memories of LHMS. I hope that he went to a better school and not a worse one, and that he had a good life. I did find a photo of someone with the same name on the internet who looked very happy, but since the photo was taken many years later I don't now whether or not it's the same person. I also  found an obituary of someone with that name who was born approximately the same year as he was, had lived in the Washington metropolitan area, and had died in his mid-fifties but I don't know whether he was the same person.

When I re-visited Linton Hall in 1980 I saw that a locked cover had been placed over the first several steps of the ladder, to prevent anyone from climbing without authorization. I also took a picture of the water tower which is shown on the previous page.

• Sometimes I would be walking down the first floor hallway and see the Commandant walking towards me, and I would greet him with "Good Morning, Sir."

One day, when I was still relatively new at LHMS and still a Private, he said to me, "[my name,] would you like to lead the third grade to its classroom?"

"No thank, you," I answered, very naively, as I would have if someone had asked me whether I wanted a type of food I didn't particularly care for, and I kept on walking, as did he.

Much later, I thought about it, and  wondered whether he really meant to order me to do so, and if so, why hadn't he been more clear that he was giving me an order, as in "I want you to" or similar words. I've also wondered whether leading the third grade was a test to measure my leadership skills for possible promotion, or whether for some reason the officer who would have led them was not available, and he simply asked the first person he saw. Whatever the case, he must have sensed that I thought he was trying to do me a favor instead of giving me an order, and he let it go at that. Many cadets would have been flattered by his offer, I suppose.

• The wisest thing that the Commandant told us: A drug dealer is someone who wouldn't touch drugs with a ten-foot pole, but would sell drugs to his own mother. (I'm paraphrasing.)

• The wisest thing that Bill told us, shortly before we were to graduate: Many of you will go on to college, where professors will tell you that there is no God. But you could be in a dark closet, hear no sound, not know that there are radio waves, but that doesn't mean that they don't exist. (I'm paraphrasing.)

• The wisest thing that Sister Mary David told me in the course of a private conversation was to look up the Parable of the Talents in the Bible. This was after telling me that I had a high IQ and ought to be doing better academically.

At first I did not understand the Parable of the Talents (Matthew 25:14-30) as I took it literally and wondered how the owner would have felt if those who took risks with the money, instead of doubling it, had lost it all. Only later did I understand it in terms of making best use of the skills and resources one has, which applies to many aspects of life. For me, this has been an important principle by which to lead my life.

This parable doesn't apply just to me. It also applies to the regimented life at LHMS which hampered our ability to learn to make our own decisions (I mention this in Chapter 24, "Punishments") but it also applied very much to Sister Mary David. She had the ultimate power to make LHMS so much better (even if the single-sex, boarding and military aspects had remained) and she could have done so if instead of spending time to censor outgoing mail in order to conceal Linton Hall's deficiencies, she had instead used that time to correct those deficiencies so there would be nothing to hide from parents. And if she had done that, there would have been no need for me to write my blog and books.

The parable also applies to how today's nuns spend time and money, as I describe in Chapter 27, "Benedictine Vows and the New 'Monastery.'"

• One time when Mother's Day fell on the Sunday of the weekend we were going home, Sister Mary David came into the classroom and told us to write home a letter to say that because of Mother's Day we could come back an hour later. That extra hour was the only time in my life that I received a present for Mother's Day.

• When I was in seventh grade, I and another cadet were called into Sister Mary David's office. There was a boy she asked us to show around the grounds: the blacktop plus the grassy area we were allowed to use. It was obvious that the boy was mentally retarded, although not severely so. I was flattered (and still am) that she knew that we were not the type to make fun of him, and did not even feel the need to tell us that he was retarded, or how to act.

I don't know whether he was being considered for admission and this was some way to see how he would fit in, or whether his parents were just there for another reason and she didn't want him waiting alone. She never asked me or the other cadet for any feedback, as to how the boy we showed around was fitting in or how he liked the school. He was my age, and I never saw him again, either that year or the following one, so I'm pretty sure he didn't go to Linton Hall. Like many things that went on, I don't know why we were asked to show him around.

• Linton Hall's highest enrollment was 269 boys, in 1965.[32]

• Sometimes there were too many cadets for one class, so it was split into two, for example 7A and 7B, or 5A and 5B. Contrary to rumor, the A class wasn't for smarter students. It was just a way to differentiate the two. I heard that directly from Sister Mary David.

• The time that we visited a submarine (Volume 1, Chapter 22) we had to go up a ladder to get out the submarine. We were all crowding around the bottom of the ladder, instead of getting into an orderly line. It got to the point where I and Sister Mary David were the only ones at the bottom. I offered to have her go before me (as everyone else should have, but didn't.) She insisted that I go first. It was only later that I figured out that she must have thought that I was offering to have her go first so I could look up her habit. I felt insulted, since she should have known me better than that.

• I can truthfully say that when I was in the eighth grade, I kissed every girl in my class. But that's because there were no girls!

---

[32] Handwritten notes in Prince William County, Virginia library files.

27
When Nobody Cares

There comes a time in everyone's life when you realize that you're entirely on your own, and that there is no one there who can help you or who even cares what happens to you. For most of us while we were growing up, even when there was no parent nearby there were relatives, teachers or others who looked after us.

In theory, the nuns at Linton Hall were there to take care of us and protect us, which was often — but not always — the case.

During my first year at LHMS, there were many things that were new to me. On a particular weekend, either on Saturday or Sunday, there was an event which I believe was called the Spring Carnival. Until the day of the event, I didn't know what to expect. It featured various rides, games of skill run by the nuns, and a "White Elephant" sale in the gym, which was something like a multi-person yard sale or garage sale. And, best of all, parents and others could visit. Not all did, and I was one of the few, in addition to the Mexicans, who had no visitors.[33]

Lunch time rolled around and the Mexicans were called to the cafeteria. There was a nun whom I did not know, and I asked her something along the lines of "What about me, I don't have any visitors."

"Are you Mexican?" she asked.

"No."

She said that lunch was only for the Mexicans, and that I was on my own. No lunch for me.

That would have been unthinkable at any of the schools I had previously attended. But if it had happened, I would have gone to the person in charge of the cafeteria, or the principal, to explain the situation, and would have been fully confident that I would have been served lunch.

But after months at Linton Hall I was resigned to the fact that to do that would have likely been futile, so I didn't even bother trying.

There were a few others who were in the same situation as I was. One of them was a friend of mine and we walked around together, taking

---

[33] The Mexicans were foreign students whose parents lived in Mexico. They stayed at Linton Hall the entire academic year; only very few of them went home for Christmas vacation.

a look at the items for sale in the gym and looking longingly at the rides we couldn't go on and games we couldn't play, since we didn't have tickets for them.

Tickets were being sold for ten cents each; most people bought a dollar's worth or more at a time. The tickets were similar to the ticket you used to get at the movies. Ten cents back then was the equivalent of about a dollar today.

There are two important reasons for using tickets instead of cash.

The first is that people spend more freely when what they have doesn't look like real money, and after you've bought tickets you have to spend them, since they'll be worthless after the carnival is over.

The second reason is to prevent theft by employees. Each nun running a game would be receiving tickets which were of no value to her, instead of money that she might be tempted to steal.

One of the nuns running a game was someone who would occasionally supervise the playground; my friend and I knew her and would sometimes go talk to her, and we went up to her that day. We chatted a while, and she was nice enough to let us play one game, the kind where you throw a ball and try to get it into a hole in order to win a prize. She explained that it was just for practice, and that if we managed to get the ball into a hole, we wouldn't get a prize, since we hadn't paid to play. That's fair.

So we did, chatted some more, and since she wasn't that busy, another nun came over to chat with her. My friend and I were still there.

I had noticed that when people played a game, she would insert the ticket into a cardboard box which had a slit on top. The box was about a foot in each dimension, and was lying on the ground. And those tickets could be used not just for games but also at the canteen, which was open. And the box seemed so close to me...

While the nuns were chatting with each other, my friend was taking a couple of practice shots with the ball, and I was thinking, scheming.

If you've ever tried to take money out of a piggy bank without breaking it you know the challenge you're faced with. My hand was too big to fit into the slot, and the box was taped shut.

Using my foot as if I had bumped into the box by chance, I nonchalantly tipped the box to its side, then again so it was upside down. I tried to shake it a bit without being obvious. I knelt down and put my hand under it; I was taking greater and greater risks. I could feel the tickets against the slot, managed to get two out, and decided that it was better to quit while I was ahead and set the box back up the way it had been. I had been extremely lucky that no one had seen me, with so many people around. Had I been caught, a paddling was guaranteed. The only uncertainty would have been how many times I would have been hit with the paddle.

I felt bad about what I had just done. The nun was one of the nicer ones, and she had been kind enough to let us play a practice game, and she trusted me enough not to keep looking over her shoulder to make sure I wasn't touching the ticket box. The thought that I would do what I had just done probably hadn't even crossed her mind. It wouldn't have crossed my mind either, if I had been fed lunch. And there I was, a thief who was so low as to betray someone's trust.

As I mentioned earlier, ten cents was the equivalent of about a dollar today. With two tickets I could get two candy bars, or two cups of soda, or one of each. I couldn't share with my friend because I would have had to explain how I got the tickets, and he could have unintentionally told someone else and eventually the word might have gotten around. It was too great a risk for me to take.

I told my friend that I was going to walk around, and headed over to the canteen.

Usually the canteen was open after school, where each of us could get a candy bar of our choice; other times we all just got handed the same thing, often a popsicle. This time, though, the side door of the canteen was open and on the outside of the canteen there was a grill with hot dogs and hamburgers being cooked. I got the same feeling I did when we marched down to dinner, smelled pot roast or fried chicken coming from the sister's dining room, and all we got was hot dogs and beans.

I went up to one of the canteen windows and got what I could get for my two tickets. By chance I went to the window where one of the cadets was working. I knew his name, and he probably knew mine, but we weren't friends; we barely knew each other. I don't know whether he was being paid to work at the canteen or had just been drafted to do so.

I don't know whether he asked me whether I had visitors or he just figured it out, but after I gave him my two tickets he said something to me like "What else do you want? Do you want a hamburger? You gave me enough tickets for that." I wasn't too streetwise, but I figured out what he meant before I could blurt out "But I only gave you two tickets."

Naturally, I said yes.

He got me a hamburger, and even asked me if I also wanted fries, and again I said yes.

I thanked him in an offhand manner, realizing that I couldn't show too much gratitude or I would cause huge problems for both of us. Now that I've thought it over, I'm pretty sure that if we had been caught we would not only have been paddled, but also neither one of us might have ended up becoming an officer when we became eighth graders.

I wasn't about to impose on his kindness by going back to his window, so I didn't go back to the canteen. I also couldn't tell anyone about what he had done and risk him getting punished for doing a good deed. But I did notice that a couple of the cadets who had no visitors also were somehow able to get something from the canteen. Had they also been fed by my benefactor? Had they stolen tickets as I had? I didn't ask.

He had put himself in danger by doing a good deed for someone he barely knew. His actions contrasted so much with those of the nun who couldn't have cared less that I wasn't getting lunch.

At the time I felt guilty about stealing the tickets as well as the hamburger. But now that I think about it, it wasn't stealing. Everyone's parents paid for room and board. LHMS had an obligation to feed us. Although parents who visited would typically bring a good picnic lunch, not all of us had visitors that day. This wasn't stealing any more than making yourself a snack when you come home from school is stealing. And at home you could get a snack openly, without fear of getting hit multiple times with a wooden paddle for doing so.

I'll probably never get to thank my benefactor in person, but I hope that he gets to read these words.

Jesus said, "Is there anyone among you who, if your child asks for bread, will give a stone?"[34] The answer is a resounding yes.

---

[34] Matthew 7:9. Verse 11 goes on to say, "If you then, who are evil, know how to give good gifts to your children..."

28
Out of Bounds: Linton Hall Buildings

In addition to the main building, the only buildings we were ordinarily allowed to go to were the arsenal (where drill rifles and camping equipment were kept) and the canteen (we stood outside while getting candy.) The few times we went to the pool we also went into the changing room/bathroom, and at graduation we had Mass in the chapel at the convent.

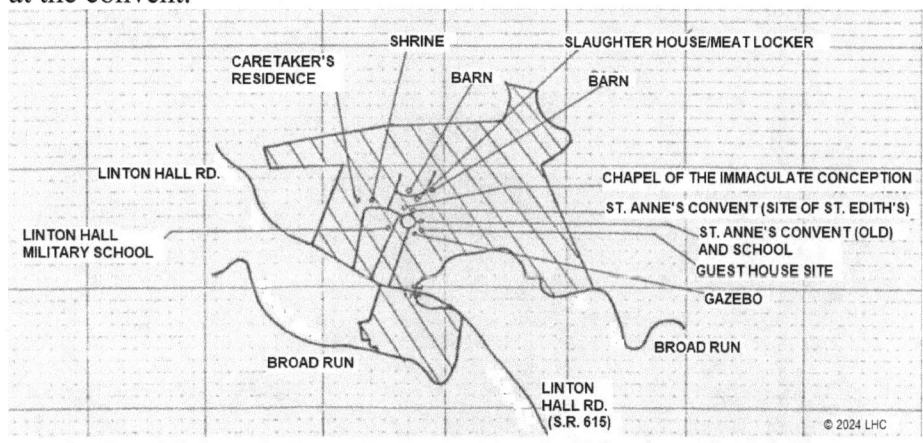

In addition, there were many other buildings on the land.

A survey conducted in 1976[35] states that in addition to the convent (still called St. Anne's Convent at the time) there were several small residences as well as farm buildings, including a dairy barn built in the 1930s and by 1976 used as a workshop, a livestock barn built in 1915 and a slaughterhouse/meat locker. Although still standing, these buildings were no longer being put to their original use, which was already the case in the late 1960s when I attended LHMS; by then our milk came in cartons, but in 1948 Linton Hall purchased 35 Guernsey cows,[36] and cadets who attended decades before me mentioned that the milk and some of the vegetables they consumed did come from Linton Hall's farm.

---

[35] Virginia Historic Landmark Commission Survey, File 76-173, year 1976.

[36] Johnston, Sister Helen, *The Fruit of His Works*. Bristow, Va.: Linton Hall Press, 1954

Among the buildings standing in 1976 were the chapel, which replaced the original brick chapel built in 1894-1901 and demolished in the 1930s, and which was rebuilt on the same site.

St. Joseph's Institute and its church were demolished in the 1960s and a caretaker's residence was built on the site.

St. Edith's Academy was demolished in the 1950s and St. Anne's Convent was built on its site.

The guest house, built in 1928, was slated for demolition in 1976.

As to the building we knew so well, it was constructed in phases, first as a one-story building, without the classroom wing and without the gym. The rooms I remember being used as offices, art room, infirmary and sewing room were initially used as dormitories, with the bathrooms in the basement. One alumnus who attended long before I did stated that initially the showers were in the basement.

The second and third floors were added a few years later; the classroom wing was added in 1951 and the gym in 1956.

Below: First phase of Linton Hall building, late 1940s.

29
Benedictine Vows and the New 'Monastery'

Women and men who enter a religious order to become nuns, sisters, monks or brothers typically take vows of poverty, chastity and obedience.[37]

The Benedictines, however, take three vows: 1) obedience, 2) stability and 3) fidelity (or conversion) to the monastic way of life.[38]

The vow of obedience is the same as for other orders. The others need some explaining.

Stability means being tied to a particular monastic community for the rest of one's life.

The third vow, called either "fidelity to the monastic way of life" or "conversion to the monastic way of life" means following the rules, customs, traditions and so forth of the particular monastery[39] of which one becomes a member. Benedictines state that this also implies poverty and chastity.

Poverty needs further defining, as it is not how the term is generally used, to mean a lack of money and goods. In the case of monastic orders it means communal ownership of goods, so that although no individual has sole ownership of any property, the property is used by the entire community.

---

[37] For priests it's different in that typically there is no vow of poverty. They are allowed to own property, but not to the extent of engaging in activities such as running a business, managing others' money and so on. In practice, Catholic parish priests do live as if they had taken a vow of poverty, as they are the lowest paid of any other religious denomination, Christian or otherwise.

[38] "2023 Vocation Supplement," *The Criterion,* November 11, 2023, published by the Archdiocese of Indianapolis. Available at https://w.archindy.org/criterion/local/2023/11-03/s-benedictines.html
Another description of Benedictine vows is provided by the Our Lady of Grace Monastery in Indiana, available at benedictine.com/benedictine-vows

[39] Although it is preferable to use the more specific terms *convent* or *nunnery* for women and *monastery* exclusively for men, it is also acceptable to use the term *monastery* for women. In this chapter I use the term monastery to refer to residences for religious orders of either sex.

This may seem like an uncommon situation, but in fact there are similar situations outside of monasteries. The most common of these is marriage. Typically the home is jointly owned by husband and wife, as are its contents, as are joint bank accounts. The couple's children own practically nothing: just their own clothes and some personal items. Although they are "poor" in terms of income and assets, they benefit from the use of their parents' property, so a child with wealthy parents can enjoy a luxurious lifestyle while being as "poor" as those who have taken a vow of poverty.

Communes, popularized by the hippies of the 1960s are another example. A few still exist today.

Traditionally, those in religious orders did live in modest circumstances. For example, many decades ago the nuns at the convent in Bristow lived in dormitories similar to the ones we lived in at Linton Hall, with a sheet hung between beds to provide some privacy. The nuns who were prefects had better accommodations, as they had a single room with private bath, which was comfortable enough, without being luxurious. The first two years that I was in college I shared a room (slightly larger than the one assigned to the prefects) with a roommate, and shared a bath with him as well. The last two years I was able to move into a single room, a bit smaller than the dormitory prefect's, but still had to share a bathroom with another student, so the prefect's accommodation was certainly not worse than that of the typical college student.

At Linton Hall we would sometimes smell the aroma of steak, pot roast, or roast chicken when marching down to dinner, only to be disappointed that our dinner featured a bologna sandwich and that the smell was coming from the sisters' dining room. So I know that they ate well, far better than we did. As several of the nuns were obese, I know that they were fed in sufficient quantity as well. Their accommodations and meals were better than those in a poor household.

I do think, however, that the new 'monastery' that was recently built is more suitable to an upscale retirement village than to nuns who have pledged themselves to poverty.

According to news reports, in October 2022 the Benedictine Sisters have moved out of St. Benedict Monastery, an "aging brick building ... built in the mid 1960s"[40] into a newly-built 46,000 square foot monastery which includes 30 residential apartments, a full commercial kitchen and dining hall, a business center including conference rooms and offices, a chapel, a library and a medical/physical

---

[40] "Benedictine Sisters of Virginia plan to build a new monastery." *Arlington Catholic Herald,* June 5, 2019. Available at https://www.catholicherald.com/article/local/benedictine-sisters-of-virginia-plan-to-build-a-new-monastery/

therapy center.⁴¹ This will house up to thirty nuns, although I doubt there are that many at the convent, as a recent photo only shows twenty-four, and I would expect the number to decline each year because vocations have declined in popularity.⁴²

The square footage works out to a little over 1,500 square feet per resident. A family of four which had the same square footage per person would be living in a 6,000 square foot house, more appropriately called a mansion.

The cost of the new building was $11 million, not including the cost of the land, which the Benedictine Order already owned. Construction was paid for with about $3 million in donations and the bulk from selling a portion of the land owned by the Benedictines to developers as well as the sale of a former school in Richmond. "The sisters continue to raise funds to demolish the old monastery building and chapel … [and] plan to create a prayer garden in the space."⁴³

The article quotes Sister Joanna, who said "Benedictines used to teach, serve as principals or minister in local parishes, but no sisters currently work outside the monastery." The writer of the article continued on to say that as part of the sisters' "ministry of hospitality" the "grounds are open to guests from sunup to sundown and offer open spaces to walk and pray amid native plantings, gardens and a prayer labyrinth."

Part of the building will be used for "ministries" such as English as a Second Language and counseling (the Benedictines charge a fee for these services.) But most people, not just families living in 6,000 square foot houses invite people over for parties, which they do not refer to as "ministries of hospitality." Often a child will tutor another at no charge, or an adult will help someone, or invite the neighbors for a garden tour, also at no charge.

Life for those who've taken a vow of poverty sounds quite nice, doesn't it?

Today's Benedictines are living a far more comfortable life (some would call it luxurious) than the nuns lived while I attended

---

[41] According to the builder, Trinity Group Construction https://trinitygc.us/trinity-selected-to-construct-new-monastery-for-benedictine-sisters-of-virginia/

[42] Back in 1991 there were 50 sisters, 43 of whom lived at the convent in Bristow; the others lived and taught elsewhere. *Potomac News,* September 21, 1991, page A2.

[43] "Benedictine Sisters' new monastery in Bristow is a welcoming 'place for all'" by Leslie Miller, *Catholic Herald,* December 12, 2022 Available at https://www.catholicherald.com/article/local/benedictine-sisters-new-bristow-monastery-is-a-welcoming-place-for-all/

Linton Hall. Back then, the nuns who were dormitory prefects, as well as the Principal, also taught in the classroom. Also, they went to Mass and prayed, but not in a "prayer labyrinth." The younger nuns when I attended were in their early twenties. A good number are probably still alive. They must have asked themselves whether prayer labyrinths are consistent with their expectations of the life to which they made a lifetime commitment.

A "Labyrinth Walk as Prayer" event involving the "ancient practice used by many different faiths for spiritual centering, contemplation and prayer" led by Sister Andrea Westkamp was conducted for a $20 "suggested donation" on September 9, 2017.[44]

Although labyrinths exist in many locations in the world, including the floor of the Cathedral at Chartres, there is no evidence that they have Christian roots, or that they were part of past Christian prayer. They are, however, a big aspect of "new age" practices and beliefs. "The emphasis of the labyrinth's proponents is upon the mystical powers of the inner self, not on the transcendent God of traditional Christianity."[45]

The same article goes on to state that Lauren Artress, the principal promoter of the labyrinth movement, "mentions 'the Source,' 'the Sacred,' and 'the God within,' which has been "destroyed through centuries of patriarchal domination, through fears of creativity and of the traits associated with the feminine.'"

The Cathedral at Chartres even erected a sign stating that labyrinths "cannot be a magical place where man pulls hidden forces from the Earth. That would be (were one to do so) a perversion of the builders/creators. For in doing so, one would substitute man in place of God."[46]

Undoubtedly there are those who in walking a labyrinth engage in Christian prayer. But that is just as true for those conducting many other activities such as walking, gardening, riding a bus or lying in bed. Prayer need not be conducted solely in a church or chapel.

So how much did all this cost? It took four years for the labyrinth and "Peace Silos" to be built, at an estimated cost of $568,800, of which $132,500 was for the labyrinth alone.[47] That was back in 2006; the cost would be much higher today.

---

[44] https://www.benedictinepastoralcenter.org/labyrinth-walk-as-prayer.html

[45] "Maze Craze: Labyrinths Latest Fad for Spiritual Seekers, by Mark D. Tooley. The Fellowship of St. James, September 2000. Available at https://www.catholicculture.org/culture/library/view.cfm?recnum=3440   Mark Tooley directs the United Methodist Committee of the Institute on Religion and Democracy in Washington, D.C..

[46] ibid.

The article I cited quotes the sisters as saying that this project will "aid those who are on the path toward a more balanced spiritual life." The article goes on to state that there are "40 'Peace Poles' honoring the universality of humanity expressed in multiple languages." According to Sister Louise Dowgiallo, the sisters "offer this prayerful beautiful outdoor sanctuary to anyone seeking a meaningful spiritual experience." Silly me, I thought that that's what going to Mass was for.

Not once do the words *God, Jesus, Christ, Christian* or *Bible* appear in the approximately 5,300 words of the article, although to be fair, the article was not written by the Benedictine sisters and they may have used those words and not have them quoted. But the words spirit and spiritual do appear in the quotes.

To spend so much time and money building and promoting a labyrinth as a place for prayer seems far detached from Christian belief, and I believe that this is something that Christians, especially members of a religious organization, should not be engaging in.

As far as I can tell, both the new building and the nuns' daily life are far different than life at St. Ann's Convent in Bristow was decades ago. I wonder what the older nuns, those who joined the Order of Saint Benedict fifty or sixty years ago think of what this order has become.

---

[47] "Benedictine Sisters of Virginia Building 'Place of Peace'" by Benny Scarton, Jr., *Potomac News,* March 10 2006, page A5.

30
Should Nuns Run Military Schools?

I used to believe that Linton Hall was unique in being a military school for boys younger than high school age, but that is not the case. In 1956, when the popularity of military schools was near its peak, there were at least sixteen military schools for boys ages 6 to 16 which were run by Catholic nuns. In addition to Linton Hall Military School, they included:

• St. Catherine Military School, Anaheim, California, founded by the Dominican Sisters in 1889. It's ironic that Disneyland, which bills itself as "The Happiest Place on Earth" would be built in the same town as a school which, if similar to LHMS, would have been far from happy.

• Barbour Hall Junior Military School, Nazareth, Michigan, founded by the Sisters of St. Joseph in 1902. Yes, Nazareth; the irony doesn't stop.

Other Catholic orders running military schools for elementary and junior high school age boys included the Sisters of Mercy (which would have been a major misnomer for many or most of the sisters I knew at Linton Hall,) Sisters of Divine Providence, Ursulines, Presentation nuns, Sisters of St. Francis of Penance and Christian Charity, and Sisters of the Catholic Apostolate. The article does not mention other orders, but it is possible that some orders ran more than one military school.[48]

This raises serious questions as to how compatible a military school, especially one for boys of such a young age, is with Catholic doctrine. Young children are impressionable and malleable, as they are naturally trusting and instinctively seek guidance and role models to admire and emulate. In Chapter 7, I wrote about the Benedictine teachings of unquestioned compliance with authority, and in the first volume (coincidentally also Chapter 7) I wrote about blind obedience unencumbered by moral scruples.

Such compliance starts innocently enough, with obedience to relatively minor, innocuous orders (not requests.) At Linton Hall, it

---

[48] "Nuns Conduct 16 Military Schools" *Eastern Montana Catholic Register,* June 13, 1956

entailed following orders when marching, or folding one's underwear in the prescribed way. I could have just gotten where we were going if I had marched out of step, and my underwear would have remained just as neat and accessible if instead of folding it into fourths I had folded it in half, rolled it, or just placed it on the shelf.

I did as I was told to avoid negative consequences, as we all did.

Most importantly, because folding my underwear the prescribed way did not raise any moral issues, or affect my health, or cause any other major problems in my life or the life of others, I didn't consciously ponder all these issues; following that rule was just a gut reaction on my part.

But such regimentation removes the natural incentive to think for yourself. It's been said about marching that "Marching diverts men's thoughts. Marching kills thought. Marching makes an end of individuality."[49]

There is a slippery slope whereby minor orders escalate and sometimes start to involve serious issues of morality, health and safety, among others.

At LHMS, morality came into play when I turned a blind eye to how bedwetters were being humiliated. As an officer, I knew all the other officers (some better than others, of course) but not once in my year as an officer did I take anyone aside and suggest that he show mercy instead of causing humiliation. Although I never made anyone wear his urine-soaked pajamas around his neck (or at least hope that I never did, and am not repressing the memory out of shame) I also did nothing to stop it. Nuns who were dormitory prefects, as well as the Principal and Commandant certainly had the power to stop this "tradition" with just a few words, but by their silence gave tacit approval.

Health and safety came into play the time a Medical Corpsman went around giving a little white pill to everyone in the dorm and telling him to take it, refusing to say what it was or what it was for. I pretended to take it, then surreptitiously spat it out. When I told my mother about the incident when I went home for the weekend, she told me that I should have swallowed it. She and I had no idea what it was. This being the late 1960s, it well could have been LSD or one of many other dangerous drugs. Today it could be crack or Fentanyl.

Long after I left Linton Hall, I was asked to do something illegal at two companies I worked for. Both times I refused, and both times I was lucky enough that there were no negative repercussions, but I did not know what the consequence would be, and I really needed the job, at a time when the unemployment rate was quite high. That does not make me the type of person LHMS was trying to get me to be, and definitely

---

[49] Rauschning, Herrmann, *The Revolution of Nihilism,* Chicago: Alliance Book Corporation, 1939, p.48

not someone who would have been promoted to officer if the nuns and Commandant had been able to read my mind, and most certainly not someone the military would want, not even as a recruit.

This raises the question as to how compatible the military is with Catholic doctrine, a question which was addressed in an article by Pat Elder in *U.S. Catholic:*

> *"Catholic school youth enlist in a military that requires the subordination of Catholic doctrine to military command. For many, the vestiges of [twelve] years of Catholic education are erased in a few weeks of basic training.*
> *Our high school children who enlist take an oath that requires obedience to Army regulations, including the Army Field Manual, which states, 'Your personal values may and probably do extend beyond the Army values, to include such things as political, cultural, or religious beliefs. However, if you're to be an Army leader AND a person of integrity, these values must reinforce, not contradict, Army values.'*
> *Jesus said no one can serve two masters."* [50]

The Fifth Commandment states "Though shalt not kill." It is not followed by a list of exceptions to which this commandment does not apply. Yet there are situations in which most people would say that killing is justified, the most obvious being to stop yourself or others from being killed.

There is a concept known as the Just War Theory, which provides criteria as to whether a specific war is morally justifiable. St. Augustine of Hippo (354-430 A.D.) was the first to define this concept, stating that war does not violate the Fifth Commandment if war is waged in obedience of divine command or following the wisdom of one's ruler or government.

Obviously, this is a weak argument, as there is no way to know whether a command to wage war is of divine origin, and each side may and often does claim, and perhaps even believe that it is obeying a divine command. Similarly, the wisdom of a ruler or government is completely subjective and, here, too something that is often believed by by each side about its own rulers.

The Third Lateran Council in 1179 A.D. did not do much to address the question, but only promulgated days when war could not be

---

[50] "Halt the Military Invasion of Catholic Schools" by Pat Elder, *U.S. Catholic*, June 3, 2015. Available at https://uscatholic.org/articles/201506/halt-the-military-invasion-of-catholic-schools/

Pat Elder is a Catholic school teacher and director of the National Coalition to Protect Student Privacy.

fought: Sundays, Thursdays, certain religious holidays, and the entire seasons of Lent and Advent.

A somewhat better argument for the Just War Theory was made by St. Thomas Aquinas who in his *Summa Theologica,* written in the 13th Century A.D., stated that war isn't always a sin if 1) it is conducted under the command of a rightful sovereign, 2) it is done for a just cause, to avenge some type of wrong or take back something unjustly taken and 3) with the intent to promote good and avoid evil.

The first criterion is almost always met by each of the two sides involved in war. The other two criteria are also generally met, as each side typically believes (or the soldiers are made to believe) that its side is fighting for a just cause, promoting good, and fighting evil.

Pope Francis addressed how the concept of Just War can be misused, saying "If thieves come into your house to rob you and attack you, you defend yourself. But I don't like to call this reaction a 'just war' reaction, because it is a definition that can be exploited. It is right and legitimate to defend yourself" He added that it is better to discuss situations of legitimate defense, "so we can avoid justifying wars, which are always wrong."[51]

A good article about the concept of Just War was published by Fr. William Saunders in the *Arlington Catholic Herald.*

He states that in order for a war to be a Just War it must 1) be for a just cause, i.e. to confront an unquestioned danger, 2) be declared by the proper government authority which is acting on behalf of its people, 3) be for the stated objectives, with no ulterior motives, 4) be done as a last resort, i.e. after attempts at negotiation have failed, 5) proportional, so that the good achieved is not outweighed by the harm done, 6) and have a reasonable chance of success. Furthermore, he states that "Armed forces ought to fight armed forces, and should strive not to harm non-combatants purposefully. Moreover, armed forces should not wantonly destroy the enemy's countryside, cities, or economy simply for the sake of punishment, retaliation or vengeance."[52]

Since the beginning of humanity, war has always been accompanied by atrocities including rape, pillaging, sadism, killing of unarmed prisoners, and other types of evil. In the past one hundred years

---

[51] "Pope calls for global cease-fire; says humanity is on brink of abyss," by Carol Glatz, *Catholic News Service,* January 29, 2024 Available at https://www.catholicherald.com/article/global/pope-francis/pope-calls-for-global-cease-fire-says-humanity-is-on-brink-of-abyss/

[52] Saunders, Fr. William. "The Church's Just War Theory (Part 1)" originally published in the *Arlington Catholic Herald,* Available at https://catholiceducation.org/en/culture/the-church-s-just-war-theory-part-1.html

Father William Saunders is pastor of Our Lady of Hope parish in Potomac Falls, Virginia. He is dean of the Notre Dame Graduate School of Christendom College.

or so, the distinction between combatants and non-combatants has been completely erased with the use of chemical and nuclear weapons and a proliferation of bombs leading to deaths and maiming continuing for decades after the official end of war, due to land mines and unexploded ordnance.

I've given myself and you, the reader something to think about, and links to a couple of interesting articles. This is a difficult topic, and I have no easy answers.

My only conclusion is that military school is more than marching and uniforms. It's a regimented world that, in scheduling every minute and prescribing one way to do each activity, stifles thought, personal growth and kills the soul. And that is its worst aspect.

31
Closing Thoughts

More than half a century has passed since I graduated from Linton Hall. The area around it has become heavily populated and traffic reports often mention traffic jams on Linton Hall Road. Every time I hear that name I thank God that I am no longer at Linton Hall Military School.

Part of my childhood was stolen at Linton Hall, irretrievably so. And yet, just as children whose parents are heavy smokers or drinkers see the consequences first-hand and learn not to use either in excess, if at all, I decided that I did not want to grow up to be just like the Commandant, Bill, or many of the nuns. I did not want to abuse my power against the weak and defenseless, as they often did. In short, over my life I've made sure to treat others as I wished to be treated if the roles had been reversed.

This is not meant as a blanket indictment of the adults at Linton Hall. Many of them, and on many occasions, were just, compassionate and merciful as well — but that should have been the rule, not the exception.

At this point I feel that I've said all I have to say about Linton Hall Military School. I've accomplished my goal to leave a permanent record of what our lives were like.

My fellow alumni, we may never hear from each other again, and I wish each and every one of you all the best. I hope that in the years since you left Linton Hall, you've been able to enjoy the good things in life, the things you were deprived of while you were at Linton Hall.

As a result of being sent there, I developed a deeper appreciation for freedom, privacy, being able to control how I use my time, as well as good food, fresh fruit, and the ability to travel far from Bristow, Virginia and to enjoy the beauty and opportunities that the world offers.

Goodbye to all, and thank you for reading about my experiences and opinions, for sharing yours, and for inviting my book into your home.[53]

---

[53] The last two paragraphs were copied from the last two paragraphs of the first volume, with minor modifications. I felt that this was the best way to end the second volume as well.

Appendix A
List of Sisters at
Linton Hall Cemetery

The cemetery is surrounded by school grounds. It's open to anyone but I suggest you call the school ahead of your visit to ask when you can visit and where you can drive and park, as schools nowadays are understandably leery of strangers on school grounds.

With the pool on your left and the water tower on your right, go north on the road for about 500 feet from the pool.

This is a list of approximately 120 sisters buried at the Linton Hall Cemetery, arranged in alphabetical order by last name. In many cases, the name *Mary* is abbreviated as *M.*.

Appendix B lists others buried at the Linton Hall Cemetery who are of interest to Linton Hall alumni.

Linton family members are buried in a different, but nearby cemetery. See Appendix C.

Sr. Irene Alexander
24 Jul 1925 - 17 Nov 2009

Sr. M. Ethelreda Altman
1911 - 1990

Sr. Theresa Anderson
22 Apr 1932 - 1 Jul 2013

Sr. Jerome Ashbaugh
1901 - 2002

Sr. Margaret Mary Bevans
1896 - 8 Apr 1921

Sr. Mary Ellen Black
30 Mar 1927 - 8 Jun 2024

Sr. Agatha Blair
1875 - 1945

Mother Alphonse Bliley
1866 - 1943

Sr. Genevieve Bliley
1909 - 1994

Sr. M. Antoinette Bliley
1897 - 1976

Sr. M. Angela Borneman
1871 - 1957

Sr. Julia Antoinette "Scholastica" Bridge
Sep 1887 - 1978

Sr. Veronica Bridge
1848 - 1914

Sr. Anastasia Brue
1877 - 1925

Sr. Walburg Brunner
1866 - 1932

Sr. Laurence Bucher
11 Apr 1926 - 24 May 2014

Sr. Martha Buhl
1868 - 1954

Sr. M. Mechtilde Butz
1908 - 1970

Sr. Rosalia Choma
14 Jun 1916 - 28 Sep 2009

Sr. Aloysia Clare
1863 - 1930

Sr. M. Dolores Cloney
1892 - 1970

Sr. Gemma Cuccaro
1933 - 17 Jul 2015

Sr. M. Xavier Dehner
1894 - 1988

Sr. Madeline Doerfler
1879 - 1941

Sr. M. Paula Dollard
27 Jan 1886 - 28 Jun 1977

Sr. Theresa Dollmeyer
1863 - 1946

Sr. Anna Dorsey
1841 - 1913

Sr. Laurentia Anna Doser
1 Aug 1874 - 31 Jan 1920

Sr. Therese Dowgiallo
1937 - 1990

Sr. M. Joan Ducharme
1904 - 1999

Sr. Mary Ann Ducharme
1903 - 1982

Sr. M. Raphael Egerer
1875 - 1956

Sr. Joseph Fetter
1889 - 1966

Sr. Gonzaga Fisher
1866 - 1946

Sr. Margaret Mary Foltzer
1913 - 1999

Sr. Edward Galloway
1874 - 1961

Sr. M. Patricia Galloway
1886 - 1978

Mother Claudia Garvey
31 Aug 1890 - 23 Mar 1961

Sr. Liguori Garvey
9 Jun 1906 - 16 Dec 1997

Sr. Roberta Giblin
7 Jan 1917 - 21 Jan 1992

Sr. M. Ignatius Goforth
1876 - 1944

Sr. Joan Ann Hallerman
2 Dec 1934 - 6 Mar 2010

Sr. Gertrude Head
1865 - 1937

Sr. M. Catherine Healy
1898 - 1975

Sr. Mary Eileen Heaps
1934 - 2006

Sr. Dechantal Heil
1903 - 1996

Sr. M. Marcella Heil
1890 - 1971

Sr. Celine Hendley
1911 - 2008

Sr. M. Anthony Hopwood
1923 - 1983

Sr. Ernestine Johann
1923 - 2006

Mother Agnes Johnston
1871 - 1932

Sr. M. Helen Johnston
1893 - 1980

Sr. M. Inez Johnston
3 Aug 1887 - 2 Oct 1980

Sr. M. Gabriel Keller
1901 - 1994

Sr. M. Kathleen Kelly
1927 - 1980

Sr. Benedict Kesock
22 May 1933 - 21 Feb 2014

Sr. Dorothy Kocian
1913 - 2003

Sr. M. Clara Kramer
1898 - 1973

Sr. Bernadette Lauer
1902 - 1994

Sr. Linda Lawrence
1941 - 2007

Sr. Imelda Leissl
1904 - 1989

Sr. Julian Leonard
14 Dec 1913 - 12 May 1998

Sr. Lucia Ljungman
1904 - 1995

Sr. M. Evangelist Loehr
1870 - 1955

Sr. Mary Loyola Lohmeyer
1 Feb 1893 - 20 Oct 1971

Sr. Berchmans Loving
1876 - 1955

Sr. M. Fidelis MacInnis
1897 - 1977

Sr. Alexa Ann MacLean
5 Jul 1938 - 10 Feb 1994

Sr. Elizabeth Manner
1893 - 1968

Sr. Martha Mary
1868 - 1954

Sr. Mary Maura
1865 - 1951

Sr. Carmelita McDonnell
1901 - 1946

Sr. Philomena McDonnell
1905 - 1990

Sr. M. Matilda Mikan
1908 - 1975

Sr. Pauline Monahan
6 Jul 1910 - 22 Mar 2003

Sr. M. Johanna Moore
1917 - 1970

Sr. Denise Mosier
26 Aug 1943 - 1 Aug 2010

Sr. Gertrude Mueller
1926 - 2007

Sr. Elizabeth Muldowney
1928 - 1980

Sr. Rosemary Murphy
1900 - 1982

Sr. Doris Nolte
27 Oct 1929 - 21 May 2023

Sr. M. Rita Nolte
1903 - 1995

Sr. Antonia Noonan
Oct 1861 - 1908

Sr. Thomas Norris
1886 - 1904

Sr. Patricia Jean "Pat" Clabaugh Novak
27 Sep 1941 - 9 Jul 2014

Sr. Agnes O'Mara
1922 - 1998

Sr. Gerard O'Neill
1894 - 1943

Sr.. Martina Overmeyer
1872 - 1949

Sr. Hilda Patrick
1901 - 1955

Sr. M. Patrick
1866 - 1978

Sr. Mary Augustine "Irene" Redding
1888 - 9 Sep 1954

Sr. Mercedes Rollins
1899 - 1979

Sr. Benedict Ross
1868 - 1953

Sr. Vincent Ruscin
1911 - 2003

Sr. Romayne Schaut
1929 - 2020

Sr. M. Celestine Schmatz
1882 - 1972

Sr. M. Monica Schnitzhover
1901 - 1955

Sr. Hildegardis Schuster
1905 – 1993

Sr. Veronica Shaddock
1902 - 1992

Sr. Agnes "Placida" Showalter
Nov 1860 - 28 Jul 1932

Sr. Hilda Showalter
14 Aug 1849 - 22 Apr 1909

Sr. Marie Teresa Smith
1898 - 1956

Sr. Justina Spangler
1876 - 1955

Sr. M. Louise Stefanik
1908 - 1977

Sr. M. Loretto Stefko
1912 - 1981

Sr. Rose Stenger
1871 - 1938

Sr. M. Frances Strasburger
1878 - 1970

Sr. Damien Tambola
28 Feb 1917 - 18 Sep 2002

Sr. Catherine Tholl
21 Mar 1881 - 25 Sep 1915

Sr. Clara Vogel
5 Mar 1841 - 27 Jan 1903

Mother Edith Vogel
9 Aug 1845 - 21 Jan 1903

Sr. Gabriel Vogel
1869 - 1903

Sr. Pierre Walker
1885 - 1969

Sr. Mary Stephen Walters
17 Oct 1880 - 15 Dec 1955

Sr. Mary Weber
1878 - 1972

Sr. Maura Wendl
1865 - 1951

Sr. Ursula Weyand
1889 - 1966

Sr. M. Carmel White
1905 - 30 Apr 1993

Sr. Jeanne Wirt
2 Jun 1932 - 11 Oct 2007

Sr. Mary Leo Wirt
1925 - 2020

Sr. Anselma Wirtz
1875 - 1965

Sr. De Sales Wittkamp
1867 - 1945

Sr. Zita Zimmerman
Aug 1875 - 1901

Sr. Henry Marie Zimmermann
25 Mar 1931 - 24 Oct 2020

Appendix B
List of Others at Linton Hall Cemetery

Rev. Raymond DeJaegher
1905 - 1980

Eduardo Facha García (LHMS alumnus)
1944 - 1954

Rosemary G. Farquhar
8 Jul 1953 - 19 Aug 2018

Virginia W. Farquhar (Bill's wife)
3 Nov 1914 - 16 Mar 1979

William Francis "Bill" Farquhar (Coach and Gym teacher)
30 Sep 1915 - 4 Jan 2011

Louis John "Louie" LeMoine (Grounds maintenance)
1 Sep 1927 - 30 Nov 2009

Kevin David McKeon (LHMS graduate)
7 Feb 1955 – 8 Jul 1973

Not listed are lay mean and lay women, local residents buried at the cemetery. There may be other alumni or staff members of whom I am not aware.

Appendix C
Linton Family Cemetery

Located in the housing development across the road from Linton Hall. To reach it you have to walk from the end of the cul-de-sac of Culloden Ct. in a westerly direction. DO NOT follow the hiking trail that goes downhill, which belongs to the homeowners' association. Instead, walk along the edge of the woods with the woods on your left and the house on your right, for about 150 feet, staying close to the woods. The cemetery is just inside the woods and is surrounded by a 3-foot tall black iron fence about 30x30 feet. The tall monument has four different names, one on each side. See map below.

John Augustine Elliott Linton
5 Jan 1769 - 2 Dec 1822

John Tyler Linton
4 Jan 1796 - 9 Sep 1821

Sarah Tyler Linton
1763 - 19 Aug 1835

Anne Cecilia Philips
14 Aug 1828 - 17 Jul 1917

Cecilia Anne Graham Philips
9 Jul 1804 - 21 May 1878

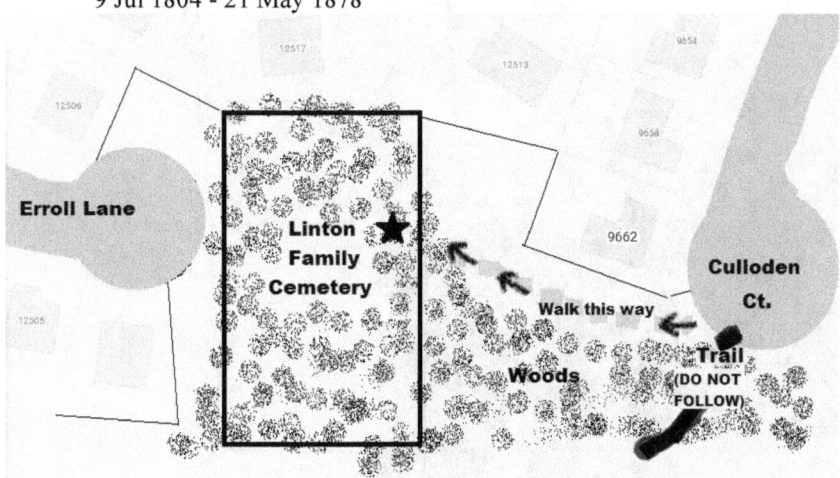

Above: The four sides of the tall monument. Actual burial sites are marked with headstones and footstones with the initials of the deceased.

Left: Separate headstone for Anne Cecilia Philips. There is an unmarked footstone at the foot of her grave.

About the Author

Linton Hall Cadet attended Linton Hall Military School in Bristow, Virginia during the late 1960s, where he earned a medal and graduated as an officer.

His previous volume about LHMS, *Linton Hall Military School Memories: One Cadet's Memoir,* 206 pages (twice the size of this book) and shown at right, was published in 2014 and is available on amazon.com.

His blog, which can be found at lintonhallmilitaryschool.blogspot.com, was begun in 2010 and the most recent post was written in 2024. He does not expect to continue writing his blog after publication of this book, but if there are any updates, he will post them on his blog.

Back Cover Photo Captions

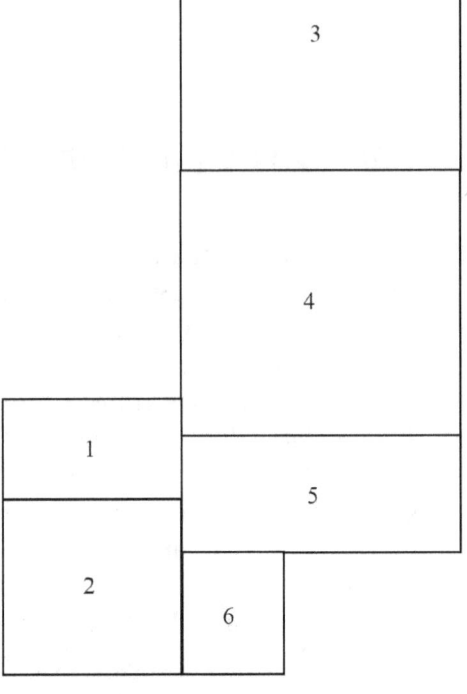

1. Rifle Club members received this patch, which was sewn on the blue sweater that we wore over our khaki shirt to Mass and on Visiting Sundays.
2. This patch was awarded the first time that you went on an overnight camping trip and the temperature dropped under 32 degrees, hence the name "Over & Under." Also sewn on the blue sweater.
3. Metal insignia from dress uniform hat. Decades before, the insignia was made of cloth. See the photo of John Phillips in Chapter 21.
4. Patch from upper left shoulder of dress uniform. The words in Latin mean "Seal of the Lintonian School in the State of Virginia" and "I live for God and [my native] Country."
5. Detail from side of dress uniform hat. The button was sewn improperly; the eagle should not be on its side.
6. Metal button from pea coat. This was a navy blue wool overcoat to be worn over the dress uniform. There were two columns of buttons, with the letters *L* and *H*.

Front cover: Dress uniform jacket, navy blue wool. The two stripes at the bottom of the left sleeve are year stripes, issued after completion of each year. As these were distributed at the beginning of the following year, this means that the original owner of the uniform had completed two years at LHMS and had returned for a third year. The uniform in the photo was made in 1954, and previously owned by someone else, but the design remained the same when the author attended Linton Hall Military School and for many years thereafter.

www.ingramcontent.com/pod-product-compliance
Lightning Source LLC
Chambersburg PA
CBHW060425010526
44118CB00017B/2363